What people are saying about

Not So Fast

"As I read this book, the Simon & Garfunkel tune kept popping into my head: Slow down, you move too fast. Because we really do. Ann—along with her family—has given us all a reason to hit the pause button, slow down, and acknowledge that God takes a greater role in our lives than all the things that fill up our calendar. *Not So Fast* is a gift to every reader who takes the time to slow down and breathe in its pages."

Lee Strobel, best-selling author
of *The Case for Christ*

"Ann has written thoughtful, realistic, and non-condemning help for families! She speaks from her own life experiences and level ground with those she is hoping to reach. Ann redefines what a 'successful' family looks like and offers solutions and insights that usher in hope and peace."

Steve and Misty Arterburn

"*Not So Fast* is one of those books I wish was written years ago so parents would be prepared for the onslaught of activity thrust upon them and their children. Ann Kroeker writes with humility, passion, and invitation, beckoning families to slow down, enjoy life in the moment, and create sanctuary in the home. Her winsome challenge to overbooked families is to reevaluate schedules in light of relationship, both with each other, the community, and God Himself. A highly practical book with countercultural underpinnings, *Not So Fast* is like water to frazzled families thirsty for rejuvenation."

Mary DeMuth, author of *Authentic Parenting in a Postmodern Culture*

"Because our world encourages speeding up, we desperately need voices like Ann Kroeker's to remind us that slowing down is absolutely necessary to find the balance we're actually looking for. Kroeker will cast the vision on why you need to follow your heart and how you can get off the fast track. You owe it to your kids, your marriage, and yourself to read this book and find a more rewarding pace of life."

Jill Savage, CEO of Hearts at Home and author of *Real Moms … Real Jesus*

"Ann Kroeker's natural ease with words manages to turn the business of reading her work into a holiday for the soul. But *Not So Fast* is far more than merely engaging and delightful; it is also and quite definitely a must read for anyone who wants to understand the joy of living fully."

Phyllis Tickle, speaker and author of *The Words of Jesus* and *The Divine Hours*

"Just reading this book made me want to breathe deeply and slow down. What an important, practical book for parents scrambling to raise wise and happy children in a runaway world!"

Mary Farrar, author of the best-selling *Choices* and the newly released *Reading Your Male*

"Not So Fast comes just in time for those of us who operate in an "ER" world—we want to be happier, richer, smarter, better, and quicker in everything we do. In a tone that is neither preachy nor scolding, author Ann Kroeker builds an airtight case for rearranging our priorities and entering the slower zone. With the help of several colleagues who add end-of-chapter essays, Kroeker blends research and anecdotes, suggestions and assignments. The result succeeds on several levels. The book is a fun read with a profound message that is packaged in a fresh way."

Holly Miller, author, speaker, and
adjunct professor of communication
at Anderson University

"If you, like me, want to become less driven and less hurried and instead learn how to savor life, this book is for you. If you long to enjoy your kids rather than race to the next event, this book will show you how. Questions for families at the end of each chapter are worth the price of the book! A must read for today's moms."

Susan Alexander Yates, international speaker
and author of *And Then I Had Kids, And Then
I Had Teenagers,* and *Character Matters*

"I've never heard of anyone with a terminal illness who wished that he or she had attended more committee meetings or worked longer hours. Instead, most have regrets that they didn't make more family memories or spend more time sitting at Jesus' feet. The powerful stories, helpful tips, and fun activities in *Not So Fast* equip us with the tools to put the brakes on our busy lifestyles and to focus on what's really important."

Michelle Cox, author of *Simple Little Words*
and *Mothers Who Made a Difference*

Not So *Fast*

Not So *Fast*

Slow-Down Solutions for Frenzied Families

Ann Kroeker

transforming lives together

NOT SO FAST
Published by David C. Cook
4050 Lee Vance View
Colorado Springs, CO 80918 U.S.A.

David C. Cook Distribution Canada
55 Woodslee Avenue, Paris, Ontario, Canada N3L 3E5

David C. Cook U.K., Kingsway Communications
Eastbourne, East Sussex BN23 6NT, England

David C. Cook and the graphic circle C logo
are registered trademarks of Cook Communications Ministries.

The addresses recommended throughout this book are offered as a resource
to you. These are not intended in any way to be or imply an endorsement
on the part of David C. Cook, nor do we vouch for their content.

Additional resources for *Not So Fast* can be found at the companion Web site:
www.NotSoFastBook.com

All Scripture quotations, unless otherwise noted, are taken from the *Holy Bible,
New International Version*®. *NIV*®. Copyright © 1973, 1978, 1984 by International
Bible Society. Used by permission of Zondervan. All rights reserved; NASB are
taken from the *New American Standard Bible,* © Copyright 1960, 1995 by The
Lockman Foundation. Used by permission; NKJV are taken from the New King
James Version. Copyright © 1982 by Thomas Nelson, Inc. Used by permission. All
rights reserved; and KJV are taken from the King James Version of the Bible. (Public
Domain.) Italics in Scripture and quotations added by the author for emphasis.

LCCN 2009928002
ISBN 978-1-4347-6888-9
eISBN 978-1-4347-0042-1

The Team: Susan Tjaden, Jaci Schneider, Caitlyn
York, Sarah Schultz, and Karen Athen
Cover Design: Amy Kiechlin
Cover Photos: Boy is royalty-free, Getty Images, Digital Vision;
all other photos are iStockphoto.

Printed in the United States of America
First Edition 2009

1 2 3 4 5 6 7 8 9 10

052709

To Philippe, Isabelle, Sophie, Nathalie, and
Daniel—fellow travelers on the road less traveled.
May we look back ages and ages hence and find
that it has indeed made all the difference.

Contents

Acknowledgments   13

Foreword   15

Introduction   19

1. What Are We Missing Out On?   25

2. What's the Hurry?   37

3. How Did We Get Here?   51

4. What Are We Trying to Achieve?   67

5. Slowing Down Childhood   75

6. Too Fast to Care   87

7. Too Fast to Rest   95

8. On Pace with Jesus   105

9. Too Fast to Pray or Worship   113

10. Load Limits   123

11. Forget the Joneses   137

12. Slow Enough to Savor Traditions   145

13. Living at the Speed of Love   155

14. High Cost of High Tech   161

15. Speeding Past Creation   179

16. Slowing Down Spending   191

17. Slowing Down Sexuality   203

18. Taking Time to Create   219

19. The Unhurried Family   229

Appendix: Meet the *Live from the Slow Zone* Contributors   239

Notes   243

Acknowledgments

To live slower requires buy-in from the entire family. Fortunately my fellow travelers in the slow lane—Philippe, Isabelle, Sophie, Nathalie, and Daniel—are satisfied with a "not so fast" life. Without their support and flexibility, this book couldn't exist.

Thanks to Don Pape's friendship and enthusiasm, I was introduced to the David C. Cook publishing "family." I'm grateful to Susan Tjaden for her gentle but firm editing—she cut the fluff and left the essence, turning *Not So Fast* into a resource that respects the time pressures that frenzied families face.

Lynn House, Julia Huber, and Sharon Stohler offered valuable input on early drafts, and the many contributors to *Live from the Slow Zone* shared insights and struggles that enriched this book. I'm indebted to numerous friends, too many to list, who patiently listened to me sort through the subject matter and often said just the right thing to help it fall into place. If I had the space, I'd list every friend I've talked with in the past two years.

Finally, I'm so grateful the Lord has shown me that by living more slowly I can enjoy a richer relationship with Him, and that my ideas and words should flow from that rich relationship.

Apart from Him, I can do nothing.

Foreword

Solutions. Isn't that a wonderful word? It is one of my favorites.

I am soon to give birth to my fourth baby, bringing our blended family to five children all together. Enough said about why I love the word *solutions?*

I could use a few slow-down solutions in my life, though to be honest, I initially shook my head and even somewhat chuckled at the suggestion that any exist.

My husband's work and ministry life call him all over the world; he speaks in different venues and writes for multiple projects at any given time, always with further opportunities for more and more life-changing work with God. Our children are interested in multiple activities, often wanting to try new things, wanting social time with their friends—and each child has nightly homework and needs showers and wants time to just relax and play ... along with needing dinner. They must eat!

And believe it or not, I have goals too. While I truly love my role as wife and mom in our family and "being there" for everyone, I also have personal goals that involve just me, as a woman. There are books I'm trying to read, books I'm trying to write, entrepreneurial projects I'm working on—and I'd like to be crocheting right now for my new daughter on the way, and nesting, nesting, nesting.

Instead, our house is on the market, and I'm supposed to be packing and purging and preparing to leave, right when I want to be settled. To say the pace is "extreme" is a drastic understatement. While I do believe our children have a pretty decent pace in their lives, mine is *more* than extreme, and my version of a "decent pace" is changing. After reading Ann's book, I have been contemplating, in new ways, our family as a whole.

I was intrigued by this book title. *Not So Fast.* Could I afford the time to be reading this? No. I'm just trying to keep up with my daily Bible reading and study group literature. Could I afford *not* to read it?

No.

I needed this.

I encourage you to read it, too. I found great insight and hope in the pages of this thoughtful, realistic, and non-condemning help for families. Ann speaks from her own life experiences and from level ground with those she is hoping to reach. The message I received is that she's "been there" and has compassion for the pains and hopes and dilemmas of managing a family to grow in Christ, to be "successful," contributing members of heaven in the real world. Ann redefines what a "successful" family looks like. She writes not only about managing a family, but about guiding and encouraging each member, providing room for the gifts and uniqueness of each, as we are taught in 1 Corinthians 12. Ann offers ideas, challenges to parents, and practical *solutions.*

Take time to engage in the suggestions at the end of each chapter. The *Slow Notes* are my favorite part of this book. They offer real help, a real starting place, and real encouragement. The individual stories offered by various contributors in this book also provided me with inspiration from parents who have made bold moves for their families or have been impacted by others who live a slower lifestyle. The examples set by Jesus, as described by Ann in this book, were truly beautiful to me and quieting to my soul.

Ann reminds me to rest by still waters. To allow God to lead me there and to guide my family in the same direction.

I am grateful to Ann for her courage and wisdom in sharing this message, and I am putting to use the ideas I found that can help me navigate more "successfully" in my own life-roles. I found reinforcement for the healthy family decisions we are already making and new vision for areas where we could simplify and create more *space*.

We all slow down at some point, whether by choice or by force. I'm doing it by choice, sooner rather than later—not as a result of the imminent total breakdown, physical exhaustion, and overload, and not because I've finally fallen apart or exploded. I'm doing it for the health, sanity, and connectedness of our family. I'm doing it to enjoy my life, my different roles, my dear husband, and the children I would die for. Hmm … maybe this is another version of "*laying my life down*" and showing a "*greater love.*"

May you be inspired with courage and hope for a life that is carried in God's current. What a desirable and wonder-full life to lead.

Grace, grace … God's grace …
And happy parenting,
Misty Arterburn

◇◁

Introduction

Although the problems plaguing high-speed lifestyles are widespread and not limited to Westerners, I wonder sometimes, were I living in and writing for a laid-back, low-key, highly relational culture—Latin American, perhaps, or Mediterranean—would I have written this book?

My husband, Philippe, grew up in Belgium. His parents and all five of his siblings and their families still live in Europe. When visiting, I've noticed that many Europeans operate at a slower everyday pace. They live slowly enough to achieve their goals without neglecting their faith, family, or health. They eat leisurely meals together. If they see a friend at the grocery, they stop and talk. They stroll in the park. Their lunch breaks last considerably longer than five minutes and consist of something far more nourishing than a microwaved burrito. In fact, one of my sisters-in-law showed me her son's lunch menu at the school he attends in France, where they live. She was to check off his selections for the multicourse meals they would serve the students. Friends, this was not fast food. I salivated over his *cheese* course.

As she and I compared cultures, I attempted to describe typical American school lunch fare of chicken nuggets and tater tots wolfed down during a break no longer than thirty minutes—a miserable contrast.

Another of my sisters-in-law has lived and traveled in a lot of developing countries and explained the red tape of many governments—just getting one paper signed by the right person could take an entire day. People have come to accept the inevitability of standing in lines for hours, however, and have adjusted their expectations. Some even plan for it, packing a picnic lunch and enjoying interactions with the people in line around them.

When I heard her describe those people making the most of an entire day's wait, I admired their sociable nature, creativity, and preplanning. And I can't help but compare and contrast with my own culture: America, the land of high-achieving, multitasking speedaholics. We're in perpetual motion, never resting, never quite satisfied. Imagine typical Americans picnicking and chatting pleasantly with people in line at the Bureau of Motor Vehicles. I can't quite picture it, can you?

I'm sure that there are times when even people in these slower cultures must accelerate to meet a short-term goal, deal with an emergency, or assist a friend in an urgent project, but because they aren't run ragged from day to day, they may have energy reserves to kick into gear as needed. Maybe their goals are more modest than ours, or they're satisfied with less. Maybe traditions ground them in a rhythm of life, where their days and weeks offer some predictability and stability in an unpredictable, ever-changing world.

We, on the other hand, assume that our days need to be filled with activities identical to those of the surrounding culture, and that our kids need to participate in a long list of sports and music enrichment opportunities in order to get ahead in life.

This default mode—these automatic assumptions—has left us with anemic relationships with both the Lord and each other.

Something is seriously wrong.

Our culture is suffering from what is being called "time sickness." Slaves to our schedules and assuming that there is no gear other than overdrive, we're literally sick and tired of living this way. Author Mark Buchanan discovered that the Chinese join two characters to form a single pictograph for busyness: heart and killing.[1] Most of us can attest to the figurative truth of that vivid representation; cardiologists can attest to its physiological truth.

Busyness and hurry are killing us.

We can't keep living like this.

It's too much.

It's too fast.

People are starting to feel the pressure. They want to stop the mad rush and enjoy life. A 2008 Pew Research Center national public opinion survey reported that some two-thirds (68 percent) of middle-class respondents said that "having enough free time to do the things you want" is a very important priority in their lives—ranking higher than having children, being successful in a career, being married, living a religious life, doing volunteer work/donating to charity, or being wealthy.[2] It's as if people are crying out, "I can't keep living like this! Stop the ride—I want to get off!"

There are people who do recognize their need to slow down and seek solutions all over the place. Without discernment, they're turning to the simplicity movement, yoga, Buddhism, and Eastern meditation. Some have embraced ideas promoted by the recently coined Slow Movement, whose roots are in the Slow Food Movement, a resistance of sorts founded in Italy to protest the introduction of fast food to a culture that appreciates lingering over homemade meals shared with family and friends. People are exploring slow food, slow travel, slow schools, and slow communities designed to accommodate slower community events, interactions, and transportation options such as bicycling and walking.

Our family is also attempting to slow down in all kinds of ways. My kids—Isabelle, Sophie, Nathalie, and Daniel—don't mind our experiments too much. Slow concepts often overlap with "green" ideas, which are becoming common enough that fewer people look at us funny. Still, friends and neighbors occasionally ask them about our countercultural choices. *Why did you ride your bikes to church? Why hang your clothes outside to dry? You don't eat out every week? Won't your parents let you wear this?* Most of the time, the kids just grin and explain that we're slowing down. We have to be discerning, however, because while some ideas emerging from the growing interest in a slower lifestyle are helpful, there are plenty of spiritually questionable ones as well.

To be safe, we need to anchor our choices in a *person*—Jesus Christ—and we need to weigh them against His Word. Otherwise, it's easy to drift, unmoored. For everyone who yearns for the benefits of a slower life, I want to point to Jesus and say, "Start here. Start with the One who offers true and lasting peace. Look to His Word. Meditate on that. Learn from Him, for His yoke is easy and His burden is light." I wish they could see that the root of meaning and peace that we're seeking is found not in a yoga pose or a mind-emptying meditation session, but in a rich relationship with the Lord Jesus Christ.

I wish that we could woo restless, hurried, overwhelmed people to *Him*.

When I slow myself and spend time with the Lord, when I invest in my family and friends, when I live out my faith attentively and deliberately, I feel my scattered self settle. I find peace.

I pray that you will find it too, and I hope that this book can help you with that.

Not So Fast includes two practical features for those moving toward a slower, more reflective and peaceful life—a life that makes room for knowing and loving God and people. These features include *Slow Notes* and *Live from the Slow Zone*.

At the close of each chapter, the *Slow Notes* section offers slow-down solutions to apply immediately—in fact, you may find the *Slow Notes* to be the most practical part of your transformation to a slow-motion family. In *Live from the Slow Zone*, you'll hear from people reaping the riches of life in the slow lane. They opened up their less-frenzied lives so that we can get a feel for their pace.

My hope is that you'll catch the vision for a slower, richer, fuller, and more meaningful life. I long for us all to focus on what matters most. I would love for our hurried hearts and frantic souls to find their rest in Christ.

If only this book could be a voice crying out in this crazy, sped-up world:

"Slow down! Not so fast!"

In Christ,

Ann

Additional resources at: www.NotSoFastBook.com

1 What Are We Missing Out On?

Just before eight o'clock on a Friday morning in January 2007, renowned classical violinist Joshua Bell pulled his instrument from its case and launched into Bach's "Chaconne." For this special performance, he wasn't onstage at The Kennedy Center or Carnegie Hall. This particular morning, at the request of the *Washington Post,* he stood against a bare wall in the indoor arcade of a DC Metro stop, dressed in jeans, a long-sleeved shirt, and a baseball cap.

Wearing such ordinary attire in such a heavily trafficked, unremarkable public spot, playing for average Joes and Janes on their way to work, he'd be easy to mistake for just another nondescript street musician trying to make a buck.

He'd be easy to ignore, that is, if you didn't pick up on the dazzling sounds of this classical music superstar. Joshua Bell—one of the finest violinists of our time performing some of the greatest music ever written, who only three days earlier performed in Boston's Symphony Hall where "pretty good" seats went for one hundred dollars—was playing a bustling Metro stop for free. Incognito. The *Post* arranged this as an "experiment in context, perception and priorities … in a banal setting at an inconvenient time, would beauty transcend?"[1]

Ah, would beauty touch people's souls? Would they respond to the music? Would they even notice he was there? Would large crowds gather to take in the world-class performance placed directly in their paths?

During the forty-three minutes he played, 1,097 people passed by.

Only *seven* stopped to hang around and listen.

Most scurried past, minds full of pressing appointments and projects due. Maybe they noticed, maybe they didn't. Perhaps they noticed but didn't want to give any money, so they lowered their heads and continued without making eye contact.

Reporters gathered a few stories. They interviewed those seven who stopped as well as many who didn't.

One who *didn't* stop stood out to me because she was a mom. I could easily put myself in her shoes. Bell was a couple of minutes into "Ave Maria" when this mom, Sheron Parker, stepped off the escalator with her preschooler in tow and rushed through the arcade. She walked briskly, pulling along her child by the hand. She faced a time crunch—she needed to get her son, Evan, to his teacher, and then rush back to work for a training class.

As they passed through, Evan was instantly drawn to the music. He kept twisting and turning around to get a look at Joshua Bell, but his mom was in a hurry. With no time to stop, she did what any of us might do—she positioned herself between Evan and Bell, blocking Evan's view. As she rushed him out the door, three-year-old Evan was still leaning around to snatch one last peek at the violinist.

A reporter spoke with Parker afterward, asking if she remembered anything unusual. She recalled, "There was a musician, and my son was intrigued. He wanted to pull over and listen, but I was rushed for time." When told what she walked out on, she laughed. "Evan is very smart!"

But Parker wasn't the only parent who hustled her child along. The paper studied the video and concluded:

> There was no ethnic or demographic pattern to distinguish the people who stayed to watch Bell, or the ones who gave money, from that vast majority who hurried on past, unheeding. Whites, blacks and Asians, young and old, men and women, were represented in all three groups. But the behavior of one demographic remained absolutely consistent. *Every single time a child walked past, he or she tried to stop and watch. And every single time, a parent scooted the kid away.*[2]

Every single child that passed the music tried to stop. Every child yearned to listen. To see the bow dance across the strings. The children instinctively wanted to bask in the beauty and delight of the near-miraculous sounds that poured out of that Stradivarius violin and into their otherwise hustled-and-bustled everyday lives.

And every single parent scooted the child along.

No time to stop and enjoy the beauty, kids; we have appointments to keep and money to make. We're running late. Let's go. My boss will be waiting. Move along.

It could have been me. At one point, early in parenting, I might have passed right by on my way to something I thought was more important. As I wise up and embrace a slower life, I like to think I'd choose to stop, that I would have dropped everything and had my children sitting in a semicircle around the musician. Absorbed. Transfixed. But even today it's possible I, like so many, would hurry past.

Those parents have better excuses than I would have had. They're working hard, rushing to make it to the office on time. Who can linger at a Metro stop listening to a street violinist and risk showing up late to an intense DC government workplace? They have to keep going, keep moving, watch the clock, and stay on schedule. There's no time for spontaneity, and no time to alter the plan to accommodate beauty and linger with it.

Taking in art, music, or stories takes time. It takes attention. Appreciating beauty requires a degree of stillness.

I thought of a trip we took to Paris on our way to visit family. I wanted our girls to see the Louvre, but we had very little time. So we embarked on a compressed, rushed, American-style "highlights" tour: *Hurry, kids!*

Run to see Winged Victory, snap a picture.

Rush to Venus de Milo—snap-snap-snap.

Quick, get in the long line to see Mona!

Enter the crowded, hot room.

Philippe lifted up each child above the crowd to peek at the famous lady locked behind bulletproof glass.

"Can you see it?" he asked.

"Yes."

"Take a good look."

"I see it."

"Okay." Next kid, same questions, same responses.

"You saw the painting?" we asked one more time before exiting. "For sure?"

"Yes, Papa! I saw it!"

And we left.

"That's it?" they asked after were out of the room.

"What do you mean, 'That's it?'" I replied. "That's *It*. That's the Mona Lisa!"

"But it was so *small*," one of the girls remarked.

"I didn't see it," said another.

"The room was roasting hot."

"I need a drink of water."

"Why were people taking all those pictures with a flash when the sign said not to?"

Yep. That was it. Those are their rushed and hurried memories. They didn't really *see* anything. Basically, they were in the same room as the Mona Lisa. That's all they can really say about it, because we had no time to linger with one of the most enigmatic works of art in the entire world. We had to move along and make room for the next herd of tourists.

While we rushed past some statues carved by Michelangelo, I thought back to the long hallway that led to the Mona Lisa. How many other da Vincis did we pass on our way? There were two side by side that we could have stopped and studied, as there was no crowd right there. I did pause in front of them briefly. "Hey!" I announced to my family, "These are da Vincis, too!"

We could have stayed there as long as we wished—no crowds—but we were in a hurry, so we scurried along down the great, long hall.

Americans in the Louvre. *Quelle horreur!*

Yet, what beauty we brush past every single day—and scoot our children past as well! They learn, eventually, to ignore the impulse to respond, to revel. They learn to be efficient tourists; diligent students hustled from one class period to another; and eventually busy and reliable employees answering emails and juggling multiple projects and reports. Over time, we schedule spontaneity right out of them. Without meaning to, we teach them that beauty isn't worth our time or attention.

Each child is born with eyes to see so clearly the beauty all around and hear rhythm in our speech; in their youth, children's ears aren't yet deadened to the music all around. They hear the mockingbird serenading them from a telephone pole. They stop to stare at frost patterns on window panes. If we would stop tugging them away, they would admire the Mona Lisa and Joshua Bell. Their hearts are still open; their minds alert. They would stop. They would linger.

They just need *us* to slow down.

Elizabeth Barrett Browning wrote a poem that included these lines:

> Earth's crammed with heaven,
> And every common bush afire with God:
> But only he who sees, takes off his shoes;
> The rest sit round it, and pluck blackberries.[3]

I used to think: *Oh, that is so true.*

Not anymore.

I've concluded that few adults even see the blackberries, let alone the common bush, and certainly not the fire of God. I wonder if the only ones left who have a chance of seeing—the only ones who will even think to take off their shoes—are the children. We grown-ups are too busy running, racing, rushing to even see the small faces lit with love and wonder, looking up at us in the busy Metro, asking to stay and listen to the pretty music.

I'm certain Joshua Bell won't be at the corner bus stop of our suburban neighborhood serenading us incognito as we drop off our kids and head to work. But what did I pass by this week? How much did I miss?

I'll never know. I *can't* know, because it's already gone. But, like mercies new every morning, tomorrow holds more beauty. Will I see it?

Jesus talked about those who see, but don't see: "Though seeing, they do not see; though hearing, they do not hear or understand" (Matt. 13:13).

He meant it spiritually, of course. He quoted from Isaiah, saying:

For this people's heart has become calloused;
they hardly hear with their ears,
and they have closed their eyes.
Otherwise they might see with their eyes,
hear with their ears,
understand with their hearts
and turn, and I would heal them. (Matt. 13:15)

Is this, on some level, a description of the people in the Metro? Of me? Does this capture most of our stressed-out, high-speed culture? Are our hearts calloused by the relentless pace and pressure of our schedules? Are we missing the beauty of Christ?

Maybe we can't see … or, maybe we don't *want* to see.

We hardly hear with our ears. We've closed our eyes.

We miss Joshua Bell when he's only four feet away from us playing Bach.

Worst of all, we miss Yeshua, as well, even though He is right with us, inviting us to know Him.

Open our minds, Lord, to comprehend Your truth.

Open our hearts, Lord, to believe.

And slow us down, to take it all in.

> *But blessed are your eyes because they see,*
> *and your ears because they hear.*
> *(Matt. 13:16)*

I propose that we practice pausing at the end of each chapter—to slow, to pray, to begin to *see*—starting right now. Take a deep breath (which is an act of slowing), and peruse the *Slow Notes* that follow. You're welcome to abruptly slam on the brakes, but it's probably more realistic to ease into a slower pace as you learn to notice—and enjoy—some of the little things lost in the blur of a frenzied life.

Slow Notes

Ask the Lord to open your family's eyes and ears to see and hear something from Him today. This is a great time to begin praying specifically about how the Lord wants your family to slow down. Ask Him to keep your eyes open to see Him more clearly in this crazy, sped-up world we're trying to evaluate. And then *be on the lookout for what He reveals.*

Consider trying out one or more of the slow-down ideas below that stand out to you.

- Take a trip to an art museum. Stare at something beautiful. Stare for a long, long time.
- Go outside with your kids and look at things with a magnifying glass: a violet, clover, an ant, some bark.
- Sketch something. Paint something. Sit with the kids to create art that takes your full attention: Try to copy a great work of art. Blob color onto thick paper like Van Gogh. Draw and shade some people or birds like Leonardo da Vinci in his notebooks.
- Borrow a telescope to look at some stars.
- Take close-up photos with your camera and try unusual angles to see everyday details a little differently.
- Write a poem based on something detailed that you observed closely.
- Borrow a Joshua Bell CD from the library. Listen to what all those people at the Metro stop passed by.
- Tell your children the story of the Metro concert, and then ask them to listen to the CD as well. What do they think? Write it down.

Live from the Slow Zone: *Ann Voskamp*

We hear them far off in the woods, just as the sun sinks further down, and I stop, like you do when the world slips up behind and surprises you, and my son can't believe it either, so we stand there and listen long and neither one of us can stop smiling.

·   The frogs have returned.

Then, after a bit, he and the dog go crashing off through the quiet of dusk coming down, worn carpet of leaves rustling as they bound through, both boy and Lab questing for game and excitement, but his little sister and I, we just stand there, having already found it. For hadn't I mentioned that the frogs had returned?

On pond's rim, she, her small fingers entwined through mine, stands wordlessly. A symphony of sound, trilling low and deep, fills the spaces between the trees, lifts us too. The light falls warm on our winter-faces, and this tattered snow still hugs water's edge. But that sound. From where? It is like it's the water itself, a looking glass of trunks and limbs, that croons.

At first, when I am still looking with everyday eyes, I don't notice them. It takes time for eyes to adjust to stillness, to slow and really see. And then, there they are, on the far side, these glinting eyes flickering up through waters cold and murky. The peepers are back and we see them.

I want front row seats. Can we pick our way across the swamp and closer? She squeezes my hand tight and across the bog we splash.

In a flash, the pond snaps shut. All is soundless. Just glassy reflection of branches pointing to that curve of muted moon come early.

She and I swish swash further out, as far as we can go. Then wait.

On this isle of tangled grass, the water slowly rises up to boot ankles. A red-tailed hawk swoops and soars, his wings motionless on the currents. Moon rides higher, tailing sun dipping. We say nothing, this Little One and I, but watch swamp's mirror, waiting stock-still for singers emerging. Bungler Lab charges up, smashing reflection of anticipating faces.

"Go, Boaz!" she whispers in a loud lisp. "We waiting for the frogs to thing!" From within the woods somewhere, boy whistles and dog ricochets off.

Again, we wait.

Then one by one, they pop to the light. We catch our breath and dare not move. Then tentatively it comes, this chorus, then crescendo, throaty yet gilded, and she squeezes my hand and we smile, spellbound.

Long we soak in these songs on golden pond.

And then, when our toes are cold and the shadows stretch to fading dark, it's time to go.

"We leaving the frogs, now?" she whispers up to me.

True, I too could stay here forever, but yes, time to go home. Things to do.

We splash through the water, feet seeking islands of matted grass. The sudden hush turns our heads. She's soundless, the swamp, blinked silent by our sloshing.

I scoop her up and tickle her ear with what I'm endlessly learning and relearning:

"Sometimes we only hear life sing when we still."[4]

2 What's the Hurry?

American families are sucked into a vortex of activities and obligations. We pile on appointments, lessons, practices, games, performances, and clubs, and then shovel in fast food while speeding along in passing lanes. Endless opportunities tempt us to fill every millisecond of our schedules, keeping us in constant motion with barely a break to come up for air. We're in a manic rush, showing no signs of slowing.

In the 1980s, Tim Kimmel wrote *Little House on the Freeway* and David Elkind released *The Hurried Child,* both big-selling books and both warning about the dangers of accelerating childhood. Yet, in the two-plus decades since those books came out, society hasn't slowed a bit. In fact, Western civilization's high-speed, fast-paced, goal-oriented life has propelled us into a state of minivan mania. We've taken Kimmel's *Little House on the Freeway* title more literally than ever: Our vehicles have morphed into portable dwellings—a place to apply makeup, manage business transactions, and attempt to sustain meaningful conversation while glancing at each other in the rearview mirror. We live out of our vans, minivans, and SUVs, sucking down soft drinks and viewing DVDs while bookin' down the road to our next appointment. We can plug in our phones, iPods, and laptops to stay connected and efficiently multitask while our kids set up an impromptu dressing room that allows them to segue from school outfits to sports uniforms without missing a beat.

We do it all with the best of intentions, but our high hopes for raising successful children have resulted in overcommitted, overextended, overcaffeinated, overscheduled, overloaded families.

It's the way of the modern world: Success achieved through efficiency, speed, and productivity is reflected in and perpetuated by fast food, fast cars, speed dating, high-speed modems, instant messaging, and video-on-demand. Technology propped in front of our faces and clutched in our hands promises us greater efficiency via high-speed connectivity so that we can accomplish as much as possible en route. Almost by default we all simply go with the flow, sucked into the draft like a MINI Cooper trailing an 18-wheeler.

Imagine that humans once functioned without watches and went to bed when the sun went down! It seems positively primeval to those of us operating at warp speed. Even microwave ovens seem sluggish to our modern mentality. We of the twenty-first century anxiously punch the elevator button in hopes of speeding its arrival, honk at drivers going the speed limit (the nerve!), and moan dramatically in the supermarket checkout line while a shopper shuffles through coupons. We tap our fingers waiting for a 2.0 gigahertz processor to pull up a file, and wonder why the flight from New York to L.A. has to take six whole hours. (Why, exactly, *did* they ground the Concorde?)

And our children grow up influenced by impatience, picking up surrounding societal values that we're so easily swept up into. Did you know that the Girl Scouts offer a "Stress Less" merit badge for Junior Girl Scouts—that's for girls aged *eight to eleven*.[1]

These days it's assumed that kids are stressed from a young age and need help managing it. They're growing up with a sense of hurry in the air; they observe anxiety in the adults around them; they hear tension in our voices. It's their early inheritance.

And if they don't pick it up by observation and association, we start imposing it on them, grabbing them by the hand and rushing them out the door because we've packed *their* schedules as full as our own.

Even within the Christian subculture, families are zooming, accelerating to stay neck and neck with their neighbors without much thought as to how the pace is affecting their souls. Peek at some of our PDAs and see a long list of activities similar to our neighbors' along with myriad workshops, studies, services, outreach events, and committee meetings that our churches invite, urge, or expect us to participate in. These things may all be very good things, but add them up and we're as busy if not busier than the world around us. Too many good things may end up being, for some, a bad thing.

In his book *The Reflective Life*, Ken Gire compiled a list of the plentiful options we have before us to fill our plates, and I added to it:

- Vehicles to transport us wherever we want, even off-road, with audiovisual technology such as iPods, satellite radio, and built-in DVD players to keep the ride from getting dull—and GPS to avoid getting lost.
- Bountiful hobbies to make life more interesting.
- Newscasts, magazines, online news, and blogs to inform us.
- TiVo'd television shows, DVDs, movies, and theater to entertain us.
- Tools and gadgets and computers to make us more efficient.

- Vacations to feel more relaxed.
- Educational opportunities to make our minds sharper and lives deeper.
- Social events, small-group meetings, and church services to make our social and spiritual lives richer.
- Volunteer opportunities to give our lives more meaning and purpose.
- Sports to make lives healthier and more fun.
- Cell phones to keep us in touch.
- High-speed Internet access with powerful search engines able to instantly locate out of billions of Web sites exactly what we're looking for, twenty-four hours a day.

With all those things filling our lives, why aren't we more fulfilled?

Gire proposed that life for Westerners has become more like an all-you-can-eat buffet, which looks good as you go through the serving line, but by the time you finish eating, everything has lost its taste. "Instead of feeling satisfied," he suggested, "we feel bloated":

> Sometimes less is more, as the saying goes, and
> sometimes a few well-prepared servings are more
> satisfying, ones where we have time to chew,
> where we can taste even the subtlest of spices,
> where the flavor lingers long after we've finished.
>
> We can't savor anything, though, if we're
> stuffed. And if we're heaping serving after

serving onto our schedule, by the end of the
day we're never going to want to eat again.[2]

We don't stop to savor. And we seem to think that a stuffed to-do list provides tangible evidence of our success and self-esteem.

But our lives are not our to-do lists. We are not defined by our schedules, activities, appointments, committees, and obligations. We are more than the sum total of all that we accomplish in a given day, week, year, decade, or lifetime.

Our worth is not measured by how busy we are.

There's more to life than what we do.

Isn't there?

Too Busy for God?

You'd think that believers in Jesus Christ would know that there's more to life than activity. However, researchers asked over twenty thousand Christians ages fifteen to eighty-eight if "the busyness of life gets in the way of developing [their] relationship with God," and according to results of this five-year study (July 2007), 60 percent of the respondents answered yes.[3]

Six in ten Christians said they're *too busy for God.*

Am I?

Are you?

Dr. Michael Zigarelli, associate professor at the Charleston Southern University School of Business, who conducted the study, said, "The accelerated pace and activity level of the modern day distracts us from God and separates us from the abundant, joyful, victorious life He desires for us."[4] It may be that we're assimilating to the surrounding culture that marginalizes God, letting our relationship with Him deteriorate. Instead of Christ at the center—instead of conforming to Christ—are we conforming to the culture? A culture of busyness, hurry, and overload?

John E. Johnson teaches pastoral theology at Western Seminary in Portland, Oregon. After spending seven years in the Netherlands, he returned to the States. During his absence, life here had sped up exponentially, and when he and his family attempted to reintegrate, they realized that our American culture never seems to stop. We lack a natural, healthy rhythm of life that allows for ebb and flow or even stop and go. He wrote:

> Some abroad are impressed with our pace.
> Americans, after all, are miles ahead in mining
> the economic value of time.... Americans
> know what it takes to be innovative, productive
> and time-efficient.
>
> But have we lost something in the process? I
> think so. We might have mined the economic
> value of time, but like strip mining, we have
> left a barren soulscape. In our hurry, we seem to
> have lost our bearings, our sense of proportion.[5]

The hurried life loses its rhythm. It just pushes and pushes with no pauses, leaving barren souls, cluttered with activity but emptied of meaning.

One year we chose to enroll our kids in a small Christian school located thirty minutes from our home. After unsuccessfully searching for a carpool to lessen the burden, I was stuck driving every weekday, looping to and from school for morning drop-off and afternoon pickup, round and round, two hours a day of dizzying driving that I grew to detest. After-school commitments merely complicated and extended the route.

That year hammered home the reality of my suburban life with kids—the land of the minivan is characterized by perpetual transportation loops to and from games, practices, and lessons. Rush down Meridian Street, across 116th, and up Oak Ridge for a piano lesson or art class before heading out again for soccer matches and science camp.

I shouldn't complain about these luxuries; we were blessed with the means to max out our schedules. We had a vehicle to carry us there, money to cover fees, and flexible work schedules to accommodate our commitments.

But I wondered: Am I living a full life, or have I simply filled up my life? Is all our busyness at this breakneck speed actually getting us anywhere? Or are we pointlessly spinning, going nowhere, with no clear direction for what's next?

It's easy to feel trapped into nonstop running just to stay on a level playing ground. But maybe we're getting nowhere—trapped on treadmills, like proverbial hamsters scrambling inside their wheels?

We need to stop and get some perspective. We need to discern what our lives are all about. We need to evaluate our choices. But at this pace, how can we think? Or talk? Or pray?

If we think, we might conclude that this is nuts.

If we talk, we'd start to reason.

If we pray, we might arrive at truth and faith.

Maddened by the motion of the minivan, my mind is foggy and my soul feels untethered. In this state of confusion and uncertainty, we mindlessly sign up the kids for another sport or lesson, following their interests in search of the one thing (or two or three things) that will ensure high self-esteem, friends, fame, and a full-ride scholarship to a Big Ten university or Juilliard. Opportunities abound—a countless supply of excellent programs and instructors are available to take our kids to the next level. If we had enough money, we could fill every waking hour with something productive, fun, educational, and enriching.

Is this the setting in which I am to develop rich, flourishing relationships with my family, friends, and God? Is there a way to meet similar goals for ourselves and our children without having to fill every waking moment with endless appointments and destinations?

Because I'm getting tired.

I'm tired of running and racing and spinning.

My kids are tired too. After a series of full-to-bursting weekends, one of my daughters requested, "Can we stay home this weekend? I just want to relax." And my then-six-year-old son added, "I'm tired. I need to rest."

We need to slow down the frenzied pace.

Stop spinning in circles.

Quit rushing.

And ask ourselves, *What's the hurry?*

Years ago, I read *The Life You've Always Wanted*. John Ortberg devotes an entire chapter to exploring the spiritual benefits of "An

Unhurried Life." I've always remembered the story he tells of calling on a friend to ask for spiritual direction. Ortberg described to his friend the pace of life in Chicago, the rhythms of his family life, and the condition of his heart, as best as he could discern it. He asked what he needed to do in order to be spiritually healthy.

After a long pause, Ortberg's spiritual mentor answered, "You must ruthlessly eliminate hurry from your life."

Ortberg expected more and asked what else there was to do. "There is nothing else," the man said.[6]

As he reflected on that advice later, Ortberg observed:

> Hurry is the great enemy of spiritual life in our
> day. Hurry can destroy our souls. Hurry can
> keep us from living well.... For many of us the
> great danger is not that we will renounce our
> faith. It is that we will become so distracted
> and rushed and preoccupied that we will settle
> for a mediocre version of it.[7]

I don't want to settle for mediocre faith! I don't want to become so distracted, rushed, and preoccupied that I marginalize God in my life or the lives of my family. Hurry is keeping us from living well. We may be literally sick and tired from the pace. Our minds are cluttered, our families are stressed out, and we sense something deeper, more serious—that our souls are barren.

If life as we're living it—hurried, hectic, stressful, and over-loaded—leads to a mediocre faith that sidelines the Lord, something's got to change. *Nothing* is worth that loss. A saner, healthier everyday life is a great goal, but, more importantly, we crave a richer, more meaningful *faith*—and we want that for our kids, too.

But where do we start?

Slow Notes

A family's transition from fast to slow not only reduces stress and provides perspective; ideally the changeover will benefit our relationships as well.

Connect with Kids

Make the most of transit time—turn off the radio and relate to the kids. Ask open-ended questions that require more than a yes/no answer:

- *What was the most exciting thing that happened today?*
- *Who did you sit with at lunch and what did you talk about?*
- *Tell me about your most frustrating moments.*
- *How did you encourage someone today?*
- *How did someone encourage you?*
- *Describe your favorite class.*

When you park the car, practice looking your child in the eye.

Connect with Friends

Organize a relaxed cookout with a family you admire that operates at a slower pace. Pick their brains with questions like:

- *Did you transition from fast to slow? If so, what was that like? What caused you to choose a slower lifestyle?*
- *What's the biggest benefit you've experienced from living a slower life?*
- *How do you resist the temptation to pile on more activities? How do you make decisions about what to do or not do?*
- *What advice do you have for a family trying to make changes? What specific things should we focus on first?*
- *How fulfilled and happy are your kids with such a slow lifestyle? Have you endured family disagreements about living a slower pace—and if so, how did you resolve them?*

Connect with the Lord

In a fast-paced world, it's easy to forget that I'm never separated from God. He's here, always available, and through Jesus Christ I have continuous access to my heavenly Father! How can I remember this reality while speeding through life?

Placing a few multisensory reminders in our paths—visual, auditory, even olfactory cues—can remind us to connect with Him and draw strength from His presence and power:

- Stick a small cross or smooth stone in your pocket. Reach for keys and remember His sacrifice (cross) and resurrection (stone).
- Set out something scented. Catch that fragrance and remember that through us, God spreads the fragrance of the knowledge of Christ (2 Cor. 2:14–15).
- Write out a Bible verse and slip it in your visor. When you pop it down, thank God for His love.

- Have your child announce, "Slow down and pray" every time he spots a traffic light.
- Keep a Bible in the car to read, reflect, and pray during free moments.
- Set your hourly watch alarm—at the beep, take a moment to talk with God.

Take time to connect with kids, friends, and the Lord Himself—because some of the greatest benefits of a slower life flow from deepening and investing in these relationships.

Live from the Slow Zone: *Bill Vriesema*

We value family suppers and always have a short devotional afterward. When the kids were little, we used Bible stories. When they were older, we would use edgy, age-appropriate devotional books to guide the discussion. Invariably, those books would launch a conversation with one of them saying, "I know someone at school like that." Sometimes we'd sit for a half hour after supper still talking.

I think that simple family time around the supper table shows how important that meal is together, how socially enriching it is, and how much you pass on your own values at that time. Sometimes it was the only time when we were focusing together as a family, because during the day we were all at different spots.

As our kids have brought their friends home, those friends notice several things. First is that when we sit around the supper table, we're *all* there. Some of them never eat supper together with their family.

They'd mention that later on to our kids, asking, "You do this every night?" Our kids would say, "Don't you?" My kids assumed it was an off night when they'd go to a friend's house and nobody was there to fix a meal, so they'd have to stick something in the microwave. But the friends would say, "No, this is how it is most nights."

Then their friends are a little bit astonished about our conversations. We always have after-dinner devotions, and guests are welcome to join us if they like or even just listen. You'd think they'd want to rush away from the table and do something else, but most choose to join in the conversation. They're a little shy at first, and then they hear some of the things we're talking about, and they're like, "Your family mentions the word *sex* during conversation? Your family talks about those sorts of things?"

So we've really been open and discussed everything with the kids during that time. I think it's huge to have that family meal together. I take it for granted, because that's how Judy and I grew up. It wasn't a choice; we were just raised doing it. I hope when my kids grow up they don't second-guess it, either. I hope they just do it.

3 How Did We Get Here?

What's behind all this rushing around? Why do we haul our families hither and yon, cramming as much as possible into each day? What compels us to keep up the pace?

Our answers may be all over the place. Some are reasonable motivations; others are questionable. In any case, it's enlightening, if at times a bit sobering, to dig a little and understand why we're making these choices. Do our choices glorify God?

Take a deep breath and join me for some self-examination. See if any of these motivations ring true as we ask, *Why do we fill up the kids' schedules?*

Because it's safe:

- The world's a scary place—we can't let kids just run around. When we sign them up for lots of things, we know where they are and who they're with.
- The best way for kids to stay out of trouble is to keep them so busy they don't have time to make bad choices.

Because it gives them a competitive edge:

- An abundance of activities and volunteer work looks good on college applications, and competition to get into good schools is tough.

- Our commitment now is intense and time-consuming, but we're hoping it will pay off in the long run with a full-ride college scholarship.

- Numerous high-speed, high-expectation activities are the means of continually improving our children, giving them a well-rounded childhood and developing them to the fullest.

- I'm not qualified to teach, coach, or train my kids for anything—I farm it all out to the experts.

- This is the speed at which the world operates, so they might as well get used to it early.

- Our kids have been able to learn outstanding time management skills thanks to this lifestyle, and those skills will serve them their entire lives.

- We've got to keep our kids on a level playing field with classmates and neighbors, so I guess you could say we're keeping up with the Joneses—or the Joneses' kids.

- Honestly? We want to trump the Joneses. We want our kids to be a little bit better than neighbors, church friends, and cousins.

Because we're afraid of being seen as sluggards:

- People will think we're lazy if our lives are too slow.

- Filling our days with sports and lessons gives our kids a predictable schedule and routine.

- With both parents working, the kids need to be doing something, too. Signing them up for great opportunities keeps them from sitting at home in front of the TV alone.

Because it's the only way to relate:

- All these activities and outings give our child a place to develop friendships with kids who share interests and are moving toward the same goals.
- Signing the kids up for organized events keeps them out of our hair.
- I hate to admit it, but sometimes my kids bore me. Keeping them busy with things organized by others means I don't have to deal with interruptions or listen to their long, drawn-out stories and incessant questions.
- If we were honest, we're using the hectic and harried lifestyle as a way to avoid relating deeply to our kids or spouse. Or God.

Because it sure looks—and feels—good:

- Why would anyone want to live a slow life? Slow is boring. Unsuccessful. Dull. Tedious. The fast-paced life is exciting, interesting, and successful.
- Boy, does the fast-paced life look impressive when written up in the Christmas newsletter!
- We feel important and indispensible when we're busy. The crazier our schedules, the more needed we must be. Our self-worth improves proportionally to the number of activities we attend … and withers when we cut things out.

- When we compare our family to other families, we're anxious and unable to confidently choose what's right for us. We feel safer copying others.
- We're living vicariously through the experiences of our children; their successes are our successes.
- The kids say they love it.

Because it's all I know:

- I'm not a good parent unless I give my kids every chance to discover their gifts, talents, skills, and dreams.
- I wasn't allowed to do much when I was young, so I'm letting my kids do whatever they want.
- I'm such a distracted and disorganized person that I keep saying yes to everything without thinking it through; I don't even recognize when we're doing too much.
- I don't know any other way than to try doing it all. It's how I was brought up. Fast-paced feels normal.
- We don't have a choice, do we?

Real people have uttered those statements. I myself have used a few of them in discussions with my husband to justify adding more to our schedule. And I've talked with all kinds of people about their motivation to sustain a fast-paced life—everyone from the lady sitting next to me at the soccer field, to business colleagues, to people on the Internet. This list reflects the responses.

Even though books, newspapers, and magazine articles periodically warn about the dangers of overscheduling, hyperparenting, and becoming helicopter parents, these reasons are powerful forces. We're entrenched in a society that can't say no and resists setting limits or placing value on a slower-paced life. We feel that we have no choice in the matter.

But we do. We *do* have a choice as to how we raise our children.

If we want to give them a high-speed childhood charging toward adulthood full steam ahead, then, sure, we can do that. There's a cost to living that way, but some people feel that the cost is worth it, as they set their sights on a future with certain goals and aspirations that they believe can only be met by way of this harried lifestyle. Many people feel confident in their choices in spite of the mania.

Or we can live a slower life. A more deliberate and focused life. A countercultural life that embraces the value of rest as well as work. Instead of letting the world define success, we can live a life that discovers a definition of success rooted in Scripture.

You may be worried: "Can we honestly seek a saner pace? What would it look like? Wouldn't the kids be outcasts? How could we stand being so different from the people around us?"

There is another way, a sensible pace that will draw your family together among other benefits. And you probably will be different from people around you, but you might find that it's a good different. Instead of being outcasts, your house may become a place of creativity, peace, and calm—a sanctuary that draws fast-paced friends and neighbors to linger. Seeking alternatives and inspiration themselves, people of all ages may find themselves wanting to experience the oasis your family offers.

To get there, we must take a long look at our lives. Determining our current state and what has gotten us here is a step in the right direction. When we understand the driving force(s) behind our current choices, we can go with humility to the Lord and seek His wisdom, direction, and instruction for how to live according to His principles and in obedience to His Word.

But it's very hard to do this while pushing our families forward on the fast track.

Over ten years ago Philippe and I attempted to boost our very young kids' learning potential by exposing them to as many enriching experiences as possible: gymnastics, music class, library story hours, park programs, concerts, visits to the children's museum, and the zoo. We didn't want to miss out on a single opportunity to raise genius—I mean, *well-rounded*—kids.

"Come on/hurry up/we're late/let's go" became common refrains I called out while scrambling to locate socks and shoes. Our oldest daughter got pretty good at hustling to the back door when I started with "Come on!" but occasionally burst into tears during the last-minute rush.

No time for an outburst—we had to go! Class was in ten minutes or the concert was about to begin. I'd toss her a brush to run through her hair, and she grew proficient at pulling on shoes and slapping down the Velcro straps as we backed out the driveway.

I wanted the best for my kids, to expose them to art, music, languages, sports, and culture, and to encourage creativity and lifelong learning, but I had the feeling that the way we were going about it wasn't working for us. We all felt pressure and stress from a life without pauses, but I couldn't bring myself to slam on the brakes. I didn't have the confidence to slow down and seek God's pace for our lives. I thought we had to do it all.

In the thick of that high-strung era, Philippe developed what seemed to be a terrible case of the flu. The ER doctor sent him home simply recommending fluids and rest, but we were under the gun: He was dealing with pressure at work, I was overwhelmed with the children, and we were packing to attend his brother's wedding. In Belgium.

Philippe improved somewhat, so we piled onto the plane and flew over. At his parents' house in Belgium, we planned for him to lie on a couch and finish recovering, but he got worse. Much worse. His dad rushed him to the hospital, where they said he had pneumonia and admitted him. They put him under to insert a breathing tube.

On that Sunday afternoon, the hospital called and urged us to get in as soon as possible. When we arrived, they told us that the diagnosis was wrong. Philippe had neither the flu nor pneumonia (and never did); he had a bacterial infection on his aortic valve and needed immediate heart surgery. Philippe, still under anesthesia, was already on a gurney, ready to be wheeled to an ambulance and transported to a hospital in downtown Brussels, where a surgeon would operate.

Stunned, my father-in-law asked if there were any alternatives. The doctor shook his head no. That was it. We had no choice. So we waited, not knowing what the next few hours would bring. I kept thinking back to the hurried moments before they wheeled him away—I didn't really say good-bye, not the way I needed to, not if that was it. I'd stroked his arm and rested my head there briefly, just to feel his warmth. But people were staring, and I felt self-conscious. I kissed him lightly on his arm and stepped away so that his parents could have a moment with him.

For some reason, we didn't wait in the hospital. I can't remember why. I just remember his brother taking us to a café near the hospital in Brussels and ordering me a Belgian waffle with chocolate drizzled on top. It was such a kind gesture, but I felt absurd staring at a fancy waffle while my husband was teetering on the brink of death. The room was dim and smoky. I picked at the food until they said we could go.

We went to the hospital, found the right floor, and followed the nurse through several doors to where I set eyes on my husband—*alive!*—fresh out of surgery. Machines whirred and sloshed and buzzed.

We stayed as long as they would allow us to linger. There wasn't much to say. I doubt he recognized us, but he was alive.

Except for the wedding, all the vacation activities we'd planned seemed inconsequential. All that mattered in those hours was life. All that mattered was the next heartbeat, facilitated by a St. Jude artificial valve sewn into my husband's heart. A beating heart.

In the weeks that followed, he gained strength and avoided infection. We passed a danger point, and it eventually sank in that he was going to stick with us for a while longer.

As I drove back and forth each day to visit him in the hospital, I got to where I could think more clearly and deeply. I started to ponder what mattered—what really mattered. I pored over Scripture in the attic bedroom where I was staying. I wrote email reports and notes home to my friends and family. I prayed. Almost losing the person I love most intimately and dearly on this earth helped me evaluate all those things we thought were so important. Suddenly, very little was truly essential. For us, all that really matters is our relationship with the Lord, and people. It boiled down to this: Love the Lord your God with all of your heart, soul, mind, and strength, and your neighbor as yourself.

Faith and family and friends.

Another day of life together.

And talk about a slow life! In Belgium our lives came to a complete standstill. We were focused on the Lord and each other in a kind of extreme Slow Zone. No more hurry. No running around in a frenzy shouting, "Hurry up!"

When we settled back in at home, our lives were stripped down to the essentials. No one imposed outside expectations or obligations on us; no one pressured us to volunteer or sign up for committees or work late hours. Instead of all that *doing*, we could simply *be*.

Those months of extreme simplicity were spiritually rich, emotionally rejuvenating, and creatively full. We were able to evaluate our schedule in light of our values—of what we felt really mattered—and fought for a new reality. Knowing what mattered most to us, we redefined success, simplified, chose a few things instead of everything, and turned down perfectly good opportunities, having learned that too many good things can actually be a bad thing.

No longer hearing me barking at them to find their shoes and jump in the car for the next event, the children began to enjoy long stretches of play in their imaginary worlds. That postsurgery simplicity paved the way for a joyful family culture and more deliberate pursuit of knowing the Lord. Now that we knew what it felt like to live at an intentional pace, we agreed to maintain the Slow Zone for as long as possible.

But time passes, families grow (we now have four children; the older two are teens), and it has become a challenge to continue this countercultural way of life. Sometimes we forget about the surgery because Philippe made a full recovery. His heart's ticking just fine, over ten years later.

A couple of years ago, we slipped back into the temptations to overextend and overschedule ourselves. The kids were in sports with overlapping schedules on opposite sides of town. Philippe and I divided up the driving, and one of us would occasionally miss one child's game in order to accompany the others to theirs. People do this all the time, but when we realized the craziness we'd gotten ourselves into, we regretted our decision. We didn't want to live that way.

During this time, while craving a simpler lifestyle again, a February snowstorm loomed on the weather radar. Substantial snow and sleet were inching toward us. There was nothing to do but stock up on milk and toilet paper and brace ourselves for the inevitable.

Neither Philippe nor I have careers that require us to endanger our lives for the good of mankind, so we drove home, battened down the hatches, and celebrated when our kids' school scrolled across the TV screen under "closings and cancellations." Being snowbound was the perfect excuse to stop everything. A forced rest.

Ah, the return of the Slow Zone. It felt good.

The day of the storm, I stood at the window sipping hot tea, watching snow and sleet slam against the sides of our house, weigh the branches of the fir trees, and coat the slides. The kids went out before the temperatures plummeted and stomped around, towing sleds and throwing snowballs. Within hours their footprints were filled again. Philippe worked hard shoveling, but the wind undid much of his work by teasing drifts across the cleared path in eerie white mists, shifting, like spirits dancing along the edges of his efforts. We were being forced inside together.

As it snowed, we slowed. And I thought back to that postsurgery rest. I recalled the peace and creativity that flowed freely. I resolved to return to this slower pace.

Over the course of a few months, we changed our patterns. We became more selective about our activities again. We tried to keep our activities centralized as much as suburban dwellers can. We practiced saying no.

The change was good. We look each other in the eyes again. We have time to relax together and enjoy conversations. We read Bible stories after meals; we pray and talk.

I encourage people not to wait for a snowstorm or heart surgery— take a break *now*. Pause. Ponder the possibilities of a slower life.

Slow Notes

Sometimes it only takes a comment from a friend, a line from a song, or a sentence in a book to deliver a message that pierces someone to the core; other times, a major loss or life-threatening event causes a family to evaluate what matters most and why they're living at their current pace.

Have you experienced a wake-up call like that? Something that jolted you to a complete stop? What was the impact? How did it change you? Have you fallen back into habits that contradict your values?

Whether you've been spared or hit by something big, dedicate some time to personal reflection. I recommend using a journal to record your revelations and life lessons. Putting pen to paper slows us down to a literal point in time and preserves those valuable realizations to ponder later.

If you're hesitant to start a journal, keep in mind that entries don't have to be long or grammatically perfect. They can simply be lists. In fact, for those who cringe at the word "journal," let's rename it "Slow Notes." That's not so bad, is it?

In your "Slow Notes," you can begin to explore those wake-up calls and what really matters to your family.

You can also think back to the long list of motivations from the beginning of this chapter and write down the top three responses that best capture your family's motivation to maintain a fast pace.

Sometimes we need to peel back the frenetic facade and study the deep-seated reasons for our high-speed life. Consider the following root causes:

- Pride (wanting to look good, be the best, or gain bragging rights)
- Envy (unhappy with the success of others—and wanting it for oneself)
- Worry and anxiety (uneasiness, apprehension, or dread that leads to fretting; unable to trust God for the future)
- Fear (related to worry, fear may include fear of failure, not measuring up, letting down our kids, or even a deep-rooted fear of punishment)
- Insecurity (feeling that we don't know what we're doing and hiding who we are behind what we think we ought to be)
- Avoidance (avoiding feelings of discomfort)

- Rationalization (justifying a choice that may be morally or otherwise questionable in order to make that action acceptable to self and others)

At risk of oversimplifying something that may be extremely complex, I propose that you return to your list of top motivations for living a fast-paced life and put a P, E, W, F, I, A, or R next to each of the three that you listed. The letters, of course, correspond with the root causes.

- Ask the Lord for wisdom and discernment. Are your motivations legitimate and healthy? Or have your choices become unhealthy or sinful at their root? Write about it.
- Talk with a friend, family member, and your spouse. Ask if they've noticed anything that concerns them in your attitude, words, or actions.
- Hold a family meeting and ask what they think are your motivations for a fast-paced life. Record your conclusions.
- If you feel that you've unearthed something unusually intense (e.g., off-the-charts anxiety or fear), consider meeting with a professional counselor.

Live from the Slow Zone:
Aimee Kollmansberger

I can plan way too much for myself to do in a day. I think that I can clean the whole house top to bottom while producing a wonderfully creative meal and ending the day with scrapbooking, letter writing, or blogging. Add to that list serving my husband and children in playful, encouraging ways … saving the environment in some small way … shopping with a plan and frugally … all in a single day? I can then get down on myself when I can't get my exhaustive list (or *exhausting* list!) done in a single day or two and as a result feel "behind" the rest of the week.

I remember, though, being in a Bible Study many years ago when the teacher said something I have never forgotten. She said that we can really only do two or three things *well* in a day … that the Lord is probably only speaking one verse to us each day and giving us a couple of things to accomplish as well. I remember feeling the heavy yoke of demands lifted and feeling an excitement to just learn to keep my day simple, to do a few things well (which means I'm not exhausting myself), and to leave space in my day for the Lord's spontaneous leading to see a friend, serve someone, play more with my kids, be creative with my homemaking, encourage my husband in a tangible way, read a magazine, etc.

When we overplan or overdemand of ourselves, we get grumpy, irritable, and view everyone as an enemy of our to-do list. We exhaust ourselves trying to be perfect, trying to be super-mom, trying the impossible … then get depressed and angry about it! No one even appreciates our efforts (and may even resent them!) because we missed doing it all in *love* … we've done it out of fear, perfectionism, comparison, acceptance, or a host of other reasons. We're a noisy gong and a clanging cymbal! Yuck!

We have all used the phrase "what do you have on your plate today?" I have started envisioning my day as a beautiful plate that can only hold about three portions. What will I put on my pretty plate today? Just enough to be healthy! I want to do a few things really well and listen to the Lord during the open spaces of my day for the goodness He wants to fill my plate with … an abundance that I can now give to others He places in my path. As I eat my daily portion from His hand of the good works He has prepared for me to do, He will then give me ideas, encouragement, and inspiration to generously give away to others as I walk the rest of my day.

Keep your day simple … just a few things on your pretty plate. Enjoy margin in your time. Listen to the soft, gentle nudge of the Holy Spirit with what to do next. Let go of being driven. Embrace grace. Look for opportunities for creative service starting with your husband and children. Walk lightly and in all things, love![1]

4 What Are We Trying to Achieve?

High-speed families are rushing toward something, and whether we realize it or not, it's probably rooted in our definition of success.

Let's start with, say, Bill Gates. And then we'll throw in Tony Bennett, Oprah, Tiger Woods, John Grisham, and Julia Roberts. What do you think? Successful? Don't these people embody success in their fields? They've raced to the top, accumulating accolades, acclaim, and fame. And, lest we forget, they've also accumulated lots and lots of money.

So we turn to them for inspiration. Who doesn't dream of achieving something similar for ourselves or our kids?

The problem, as you might suspect, is that we're using the world's pattern of success. In school hallways, magazines, TV shows, and ads, our families are bombarded with incessant visuals and voices promoting entertainment, ease, affluence, consumption, and acquisition.

The world claims that the fast track to success requires winning the final game and taking home the trophy, being well educated and well connected, landing a prestigious job, cashing an impressive paycheck, and building a gorgeous home. Both kids and adults may be tempted to believe that success has to do with popularity, happiness, health, leisure, and comfort—and why not throw in leadership skills or even fashion savvy? If we're pressed for time, we could sum up success in four words: wealth, power, beauty, and fame.

I appreciated what Tim Kimmel wrote in his book *Raising Kids for True Greatness*. He said that if we're aiming for the world's definition of success—wealth, power, beauty, and fame—we're aiming too low.[1]

The Bible calls us to higher heights—and yet moving up in the kingdom requires a descent of sorts that surely, to the world, looks like underachievement or, to borrow a biblical term, foolishness.

Moses comes to mind—his true greatness didn't come through his status in Pharaoh's family, as he presumably enjoyed all the perks that BC Egyptian wealth and power could afford; rather, he found the path to greatness the super-slow way—after a self-imposed, forty-year sojourn as a shepherd, he crept up to a burning bush and received word that God would use him for His purposes (Ex. 2–4). As a servant of the Lord who obeyed and belonged to Him completely, Moses was a friend of God and spoke with Him face-to-face. He became great when he was completely humbled before the one true, great God.

Or take the apostle Paul. Back when he was Saul, he had plenty to brag about—he was on the fast track to first-century success among his fellow Jews. Then he took off toward Damascus. Around noon, he was stopped in his tracks as Jesus called him to serve and be a witness, and Paul immediately left everything he knew, devoting himself completely to the Lord Jesus Christ, whom he had previously been persecuting. Whatever was considered by others to be successful, Paul willingly abandoned for the sake of Christ, serving as a missionary and church planter and producing a substantial chunk of our New Testament. That's *greatness*.

Most of us understand that the Bible's call to greatness doesn't look at all like the world's success—that it is, in fact, pretty much the opposite. Jesus told His disciples, "Whoever wants to become great among you must be your servant, and whoever wants to be first must be your slave—just as the Son of Man did not come to be served, but to serve, and to give his life as a ransom for many" (Matt. 20:26–28). Another time He had a little child stand among them. "Whoever welcomes this little child in my name welcomes me," He said, "and whoever welcomes me welcomes the one who sent me. For he who is least among you all—he is the greatest" (Luke 9:48).

To become great, be a servant.

To be first, be a slave.

He who is least is the greatest.

It's a slower approach, not racing to get to the front of the line or stepping on people en route. It's a willingness to slow down and pay attention, to look outside oneself.

How does it work into our day-to-day pace? Our choices? Our priorities?

And how often and how well do we remind our kids of this truth?

Our kids need to know that the world's fast-track approach to success is centered on self—self-improvement, self-satisfaction, self-reliance, and plain old selfishness.

And they need to hear that the Bible's call to success is in direct contrast to the world's: it is self*less*, centered on God the Father and His Son, Jesus Christ. Do they see in our everyday choices that a life of true success—of Christlike greatness—depends upon a daily yielding to Jesus as Lord? Do our children know that we trustingly lay at the foot of the cross our plans, goals, and aspirations—along with the goals and dreams that we have for them?

Years ago, my friend Ruth told me about how her brother's family went through a time of illness and suffering. She asked him how he could stay so faithful and positive in the midst of it. He said, "The way I see it, it's no longer I, but Christ lives in me. This is *His* life, not mine. Who am I to question how He chooses to live His life?" That story has stuck with me for over a decade. He had submitted so literally and completely to the Lord that he accepted the suffering as Jesus' decision for His own life.

Our life is His life to live as He pleases. That's the radical, countercultural life we can embrace: a life that's completely Christ's. He bought it with the price of His blood, shed on the cross, and we can freely give it to Him to live however and at whatever pace He chooses. When we live that way, success becomes whatever Jesus Christ chooses for us.

Some days I wake up, and I'm not sure *I'm* ready to be that radically His, let alone tell my children that this is the life of a disciple. Sometimes I'm not ready to give up my material dreams for them. To live completely for Christ—to really submit daily and be His eager servant—is countercultural to the extreme.

My gerbil-spinning daily scramble for meaning is so pathetic compared with a life absolutely abandoned to Jesus Christ.

Am I teaching my children to worry about what others think about them, to grab the brass ring, to edge out others to get to the top, to frantically fill their days, doing whatever it takes to win?

Or am I urging them to seek the Lord above all else?

Do I emphasize their GPA so much that they consider cheating to get an A, or do I urge them to do all that they do for the glory of God (1 Cor. 10:31) and release them from the pressure to cut corners, perform, or achieve for achievement's sake? Do I encourage them with Paul's words to the Colossians, "And whatever you do, whether in word or deed, do it all in the name of the Lord Jesus, giving thanks to God the Father through him" (Col. 3:17)? Do I live my own life so that everything that I aim for—everything that I think, do, say, plan, eat, drink, or buy—I do in the name of the Lord Jesus? I can't live that way perfectly every day, but will they recognize my central commitment to loving the Lord with all that I am? I hope so.

But the messages of the world are so loud and seem so true and appealing, to kids and grown-ups alike. Those lies tempt. They kick me into high gear again, frantic and frenzied, chasing after the wind. That pattern of success is tiring and fruitless.

Give me a biblical vision of success any day.

It's not easy to live out, but, centered and slower, living the greatness to which the Bible calls me helps downplay the crazy craving for the stuff of the world that sends me racing off in all directions, and keeps me from pointing my kids to do the same.

Slow Notes

Pull out your journal and write "Success" at the top of a page.

- List words that honestly mean "success" to you. Don't give a "right" answer; be honest about how you're actually living it. Draw it, if you like.

- Without offering any explanation, teaching, or leading words, ask your child, "What do you think success is?" Without correcting, praising, or judging, write down the response.
- Ask your spouse the same thing. Write down the response.
- What do you think of those responses? Were you pleased? Surprised? Hopeful? Disturbed?
- How have your definitions of success affected your speed of life?
- Now describe your reaction to the passages presented in this chapter. Do you agree with them? Record your own biblical definition of success.
- How would a biblical view of success change your daily pace?
- Ephesians 2:10 says that we're created to do good works. What kinds of good works do you feel that the Lord has asked you to do individually and as a family? Ask Him to show you the next assignment He has for you that will fulfill His desires and purpose.
- List several things you can do to remember the Lord's authority and right to ownership of your life.
- Read Philippians 2:3–11 aloud as a family. Discuss what it says about doing away with the selfish ambition of the success-driven life.

Live from the Slow Zone: *Bill Vriesema*

There's a principle that the amount of stress you experience is proportional to how far you've strayed from your values. When I ask myself why I'm stressed, I find that too much of whatever I value isn't there.

So when people are signing their kids up for everything, worried that they won't have an edge, I question the driving value: Is it success? Money? And are they trying to replicate themselves in their child? Most of us don't want our kids to be replicated *exactly* as we are—we want them to be spared our faults and baggage. So we try to adjust.

But how did that parent even have the ability to think and conclude, "I want this change for my child from my childhood"? They had to slow down and make time to think. They had to engage their minds to make a value choice. Unfortunately, a lot of people aren't slowing down enough and are making value choices a little bit blindly. Some people think that by getting their kids involved in lots of activities, they're going to get ahead. But if they take the time to think further down the line, they'll see that some of the most brilliant, well-educated people aren't necessarily the ones who are contributing to society or are even happy.

Scores coming out of high school do matter, because they allow your child to get college scholarships. And some of the choices that people make do allow their kids to get into that better college. But once they've gotten into the better college and landed the better job, the question is, are they happy? Have they met their values? Or are they repeating the whole stress cycle all over again? If their goal is to have their child be very successful as the world sees it, they're probably going about it the right way and will achieve those goals. But are they truly contributing to society? Are they passing on their values to their children? It really boils down to your final value.

God said in the Bible that our ways are not His ways, and sometimes our *values* are not His values. He doesn't care if we have three cars in the garage and a boat and an extra home—He cares what we're giving back to other people. Where are those values best learned? In the echelons of higher education? At the best colleges in the world? Or are they best learned in the nesting ground of a family? Are they learned while growing up together and interacting around the supper table? I believe people skills and the emotional intelligence needed to be successful in life are best developed in the slower pace of home.

5 Slowing Down Childhood

Imagine your child wrote a college application essay that began something like this:

"I lived a deliciously slow childhood. My siblings and I took long walks in the woods and caught fireflies in jars in the summer. We would wade in the creek and stare at pond skaters skimming the water's surface. In winter, after tromping over piles of snow, we curled up in front of the fireplace with books and read all afternoon with no noises other than the subtle swoosh of a page being turned. We prayed often—at dinner and bedtime and anytime we felt the urge to worship or be thankful or ask for help. By draping sheets over a clothes line, we imagined we were in an army barracks, fighting in the Revolutionary War. Life was slow and sweet, full of spontaneity and creativity, embracing a natural approach to learning as part of everyday life, and mingling reading and play with meaningful work."

What do you suppose the Harvard admissions office would say to that? Would they dismiss it as a poetic framing of ridiculous underachievement, or would they celebrate it? Would they embrace someone who benefited from a real childhood, full of wonder and in touch with nature? Would they believe that a freer, less-structured upbringing breeds creative problem-solvers who can move into society as energetic leaders because they weren't burned out by high-speed, high-pressured, highly scheduled childhoods? Would they appreciate a life rooted in faith?

I use Harvard as shorthand for any elite college or university—it could just as easily be the College of William & Mary, Yale, Emory, Davidson, Pepperdine, Columbia, or USC. Top schools probably still expect an aggressive résumé reflecting measurably high achievers groomed for the fast track. Students used to being pushed and continually "perfected" will more likely survive the grueling, taxing academic pressures they'll face throughout the four or so years on their campus.

And yet, the former dean of students at Harvard sent out a letter to all incoming freshmen, an essay entitled, "Slow Down: Getting More out of Harvard by Doing Less." In it, Dr. Harry Lewis wrote:

> You may succeed more fully at the things that will be most important to you if you enter Harvard with an open mind about the possibilities available to you, but gradually spend more of your time on fewer things you discover you truly love. You may balance your life better if you participate in some activities purely for fun.... But the most important thing you need to master is the capacity to make choices that are appropriate to you, recognizing that flexibility in your schedule, unstructured time in your day, and evenings spent with your friends rather than your books are all, in a larger sense, essential for your education.... You are more

> likely to sustain the intense effort needed
> to accomplish first-rate work in one area if
> you allow yourself some leisure time, some
> recreation, some time for solitude, rather than
> packing your schedule with so many activities
> that you have no time to think about why you
> are doing what you are doing.[1]

Call me crazy, but doesn't my hypothetical essay-opener sound a little like it was written by a person who already enjoyed some of Dr. Lewis's recommendations? Our student spent time on fewer activities that she discovered she truly loved and allowed for some leisure time, recreation, and solitude in order to sustain effort necessary for first-rate work.

Let's just imagine that the student's application continued to include good grades and some solid examples of service and leadership in her high school years—neither a breathtakingly long list nor one that begins with a program for gifted preschoolers, but one that highlights a few focused pursuits. This person seems to have lived a balanced and healthy life. Her parents chose not to pack her childhood chock-full of continuous opportunities for "improvement." Instead, she was raised with time and space to savor life, connect with family and friends, think enough to form opinions, and develop key interests that may last a lifetime.

Thanks to her simpler childhood, our hypothetical student probably had more time to relate to people. She'll likely connect with peers and professors on campus and exhibit healthy emotional intelligence on the job. In her slower, steadier childhood, she may have had opportunities to deepen her faith and turn to Christ as her anchor throughout life.

To get into Harvard (or Yale or UVA or Davidson), do our children *have* to live a high-strung, high-speed, high-expectation lifestyle? How would those school recruiters respond to a simpler résumé, like our sample student's?

We'd have to send it in and see. But Harvard leaders report their concern at seeing students arrive on campus to begin their college career already burned out from their high school years. That's part of what prompted Lewis's essay "Slow Down," and even Lewis's successor, Benedict Gross, has written to students: "I hope you will learn to pace yourself."[2]

If that weren't enough to question the fast track, an article from the Harvard College Admissions office online explains that, while many students cope well with pressure and even thrive under it, it's common to encounter successful students who have spent years acquiring credentials and "prizes" stepping back to wonder, "Is it all worth it?" They write:

> Professionals in their thirties and forties—
> physicians, lawyers, academics, business people
> and others—sometimes give the impression
> that they are dazed survivors of some bewilder-
> ing life-long boot-camp. Some say they ended
> up in their profession because of someone else's
> expectations, or that they simply drifted into
> it without pausing to think whether they really
> loved their work. Often they say they missed

their youth entirely, never living in the present,
always pursuing some ill-defined future goal.[3]

I don't want to devise a life that leaves my child feeling that he
was enrolled in "some bewildering life-long boot-camp" and missed
his youth entirely. I don't want him to devote himself to "pursuing
some ill-defined future goal."

Life is short. Time flies. It seems that if you blink, your child
goes from toddling with a sippy cup in hand to signing up for driver's
ed, a Starbucks mug propped in the drink holder. Why speed it up?
Why rush? Why hurry through the precious years of youth, when
ideas are budding and curiosity is insatiable?

My friend Julia took her son, Morgan, to a weeklong basketball
camp when he was six. Another parent, a dad, asked, "Do you have
him signed up for the baseball camp, too?"

"No," she replied. "He'll probably get interested in baseball in a
couple of years."

He shook his head. "It'll be too late," he warned her.

"Too late? What do you mean?"

"By that time, the other kids will be too advanced for him to
catch up."

Julia felt a hint of hesitation—should she go ahead and sign up
Morgan? What if he ended up falling way behind others his age?—
but she resisted. She trusted her instincts, and instead of signing
him up for baseball after basketball camp was over that summer,
Julia encouraged him to enjoy free play and run barefoot in the sun-
warmed grass. A couple of nights a week, the whole family went out
to the cul-de-sac after dinner and took turns hitting, fielding, and

pitching. "Sometimes the neighbor kids would watch us," she said. "They would creep ever closer and every once in awhile ask if they could join us. In our neighborhood, you would never see a mom, dad, and teenaged sister playing baseball with the youngest member of the family, so we must have seemed odd. Morgan's skills the first summer were poor, but magically, the next summer he usually connected bat to ball and could really send it! I guess some family encouragement and the natural development of hand-eye coordination at that age was all that our sensitive boy needed."

My friend Judy Vriesema points out that kids' opportunities to discover their special gifts are *lifelong*. "We think that kids have to be exposed to everything in childhood in order to be good at it, but it's just not true. If it's meant to come out of them, *God* will bring it out." She uses herself as exhibit A. "Look at me—I never gardened when I was young. Oh, I helped weed my parents' vegetable garden begrudgingly, but as an adult, I *love* gardening. God is good; He'll give you new gifts as you go. There's not just this narrow season of life in which we can explore our interests and gifts. It's not all in childhood."

Slow down. Let your daughter build an obstacle course through the living room with pillows. Offer ideas without adding excessive structure. Read books and Scripture. Play games. Talk. Listen. Laugh. Love. Learn.

Give your kids a childhood.

Inner Slow

We can work on slowing down on the outside—it's a tangible place to start. But even if we manage to simplify our schedules, adjust our rapid speech patterns, and begin to look our children in the eyes, we may struggle with our *inner* speed.

We need to slow down on the *inside*.

Our hearts and minds—even our souls—can remain jittery and anxious, even when the pace all around us is relaxed. Have you ever met people who can't downshift during a vacation? Even with a low-key schedule and relaxed pace, they're edgy. They check their BlackBerrys every few minutes and want to *do* something. Even if they resolve to cut back and live a simpler life logistically, they continue to feel agitated.

Then there are those who seem to glide through everything with an air of calm confidence. Have you seen them? Look at their eyebrows—nothing's furrowed or tense. Kids can be weaving through their legs, spilling milk, and dribbling crumbs all over their freshly mopped floor, and they just go with the flow. Regardless of circumstances, they seem to dwell in a place of soulful serenity.

Oh, to be born with such inner tranquility!

I'm not naturally calm or composed. When my kids were tiny and demands of motherhood were nonstop, I was usually frazzled and snippy, on track to developing chronic stress symptoms. Recognizing my hopelessly frenzied state of being, I managed to set aside a few moments with the Lord in the midst of motherhood. I would pull out a journal and pour out my heart to God, begging His Holy Spirit to sustain and change me. As far as I could tell, though, no big shifts to my internal speed took place.

Then one day my girls and I were heading to a mother's-day-out program. We were late. Normally I would have felt aggravated by their dawdling at the door, tugging on my clothes, posing question after question.

That morning, however, in spite of external kid-chaos, I was relaxed. Calm. Peace pervaded. My naturally agitated self was unruffled, and I spoke in soft, loving tones—I was just the kind of tranquil mom I had always longed to be. As I held the door, a friend of mine paused on her way out, remarking, "There you are with all your kids, and you're so calm! What's your secret?"

Surprised, I replied, "I … well, I don't know."

"I don't know how you do it!" she continued. "I'm going nuts trying to get my two kids in there, but you look totally relaxed, and you've got *three.*"

As she said good-bye and continued to the parking lot, I thought, *Is this me? I'm the nagging, stressed-out mom—not the calm, relaxed one!*

Ah … my desperate prayers had been answered; for at least one morning, I had been given this glorious gift of soulful serenity. The Holy Spirit was at work, and I was the humble recipient of a fruit-of-the-Spirit moment—a pileup of love, joy, peace, patience, kindness, goodness, faithfulness, gentleness, and self-control.

There's nothing like a little helplessness to open you up for God's work in your life.

Whether external or internal, the blessings and benefits of a slower life aren't from my own efforts—they depend on and flow from the Lord Himself.

He got through to me. He changed me and is still changing me, and I'm so grateful—I have cranky days, but overall, my precious kids are having a childhood. They've run through sun-warmed grass on summer afternoons. And I've sat and watched them from the porch, praying, asking the Lord to search me and know my heart; to test me and know my anxious thoughts; to see if there's any offensive way in me and lead me in the way everlasting.

He has, in fact, led me beside slow, still waters. And my soul is being restored.

What is slow?

Whatever it is, it's difficult—if not impossible—to achieve … apart from Christ.

Slow Notes

I already recommended that you begin keeping a personal Slow Notes journal. Now I'd like to suggest a *family* journal: collective Slow Notes where your entire family records struggles, revelations, and insight. Ask and record responses to the following:

- On a scale of one to ten, with one being turtle-slow and ten being Indy 500-fast, how fast is our family usually operating?
- What's our current pace of life and what effect is it having on each of us?
- Let's list our weekly activities.
- How has our pace of life been affecting our souls, faith, or relationship with the Lord?
- What's our motivation to keep up this pace?
- Let's describe the slower life we're craving. Describe actual days. How would they feel? What would we do? What wouldn't we do?

Try these ideas for regular family devotions:

- Launch with a fun "ice breaker" question.
- Ask what stands out from the week. As concerns come up, discuss them and pray right away.
- Ask for insight, trusting the Lord to open your eyes that you might see wonderful things in His law (Ps. 119:18).
- Read a Bible story or passage out loud.
- Have young children retell it in some way. They can:
  - Draw the scene.
  - Act it out.
  - Use puppets or plastic figures such as Little People or Playmobil.
  - Dictate to an older sibling or parent.
- Ask questions pertaining to the passage:
  - What can we learn about God from the story?
  - What can we learn about human nature?
  - Does this passage offer ideas for how to live … or how not to live?
- Ask genuine questions that respect everyone's intelligence, and expect some interesting discussion. Don't underestimate the child's comprehension. Write down insights.
- Pray, expressing dependence on the Lord. End with each person offering a word of thanks.

Over time, add your own ideas for illustrating a passage in some memorable way—one time we had a tug-of-war game in the living room to illustrate Paul's (and our) struggle with sin (Rom. 7)—or keep it simple. Object lessons are great, but it's also healthy for kids to see that studying and interacting with the dynamic Word of God can be a simple, straightforward, everyday process.

Live from the Slow Zone: *Trish Southard*

So many kids from high-achieving families in Tucson have absolutely no open time. It's like their minds are cluttered—and they get so stressed out! They feel like they have nothing in their life that they control because their parents are controlling every minute of their day. How can they possibly develop their own ideas of what they're good at? And how can the parent even see what her child excels at if she's always pushing, pushing, pushing? How can children have time to sketch a picture or be creative in their rooms? Those things will never happen if they never have any open time.

My daughter, Sabrina, is friends with an eleven-year-old girl whose mom had her playing six hours of tennis every day this summer so that she could travel and be in tournaments this year. In fact, a lot of kids are in tennis camps all summer long, even though it's 105 degrees and the sun's blazing down. They get sunburned because they don't want their skills to decline. Why on earth would we have our kid go out in the blazing heat all summer to attend a tennis camp here in Arizona?

Well, that friend of Sabrina's got so badly injured that her shoulder is out. But she's still playing tennis! What's that all about? That little girl is probably going to have shoulder pain in her fifties because of an injury from overwork trying to please her parents when she was eleven. Why wouldn't someone think that something's wrong with that?

Instead of signing Sabrina up for those summer camps, we kept her at home. She did great in the little tournament last week, so I guess her skills didn't suffer by resting and reading books and swimming. But, you know, we honestly wouldn't have minded if they had.

6 Too Fast to Care

I consider myself to be a compassionate person—if I came across someone in need, I like to think I'd stop and help out in any way that I could. In fact, most Christians think of themselves as caring people, willing to show love and goodwill to others. What could desensitize us? What could possibly change us into people who could just pass right by when someone obviously needs assistance?

Back in 1970, two researchers wanted to explore this question. To do so, they recruited several people preparing for the ministry to participate in a study. The volunteers were assigned a message to prepare—some of them were told to talk on the jobs for which a seminary student would be effective, while others were assigned the parable of the good Samaritan.

After responding to a questionnaire, the seminarians were asked to report to another building to give their talks. The schedule was such that some of them were placed in a high-hurry situation, some in a medium-hurry situation—and others were in no hurry at all, having been given plenty of time to arrive at the follow-up location.

While in transit, the subjects had to cut through an alley and pass a slumped "victim," placed there by the researchers. According to a personal analysis of the study provided by Richard Beck, associate professor of psychology at Abilene Christian University, the plant was "sitting slumped against the wall, head down and eyes closed.... Basically, they [sic] showed signs of abdominal pain. As the seminarians passed, the key variable was recorded: Would they stop to check on the groaning person?"[1] Surely they all would, or most of them? After all, they were training for a helping profession, and certainly the ones who had the lessons of the Good Samaritan at the front of their minds would stop and see what they could do to assist. They'd be aware of the situational irony and concerned about the hypocrisy. They would stop … wouldn't they?

Here's how it turned out:

Overall, only 40 percent offered some help to the staged victim. But look a little closer—consider how the hurry variable affected the results:

> Low hurry—*63 percent* stopped to help.
> High hurry—*10 percent* stopped to help.[2]

Only 10 percent of the students who were in a big rush bothered to stop! In fact, Beck explained that some of the seminarians literally stepped over the slumped person as they rushed to deliver their sermons on the Good Samaritan.[3]

Another report noted that some subjects who didn't stop to help did at least appear anxious when they showed up at the second site. That same report went on, however, to offer a provocative statement: Maybe "ethics become a luxury as the speed of our daily lives increases."[4]

We're going too fast to do the right thing.

That's sobering. Does a fast-paced life shrivel our hearts and shrink our souls? Does a frantic schedule wreak havoc with our willingness to show compassion?

Will our children gradually learn to harden their hearts by watching us regularly harden ours toward a plea or a cry—just so that we can reach a restaurant or a lesson or a practice on time? What are we passing on to the next generation—a legacy of love and service, practiced in a family that lives slow enough to take time to notice and respond? Or are we modeling a life of hypocrisy, passing along nothing more powerful than the importance of arriving on time, as we call out, "Hurry! There's no time for that—we've got to go!"

As an everyday rule, it's a good practice to arrive on time to meetings and appointments—a habit that demonstrates respect for whoever is organizing, leading, or in attendance at the function.

But if a nonstop, overly hurried life leaves so little room for the unexpected, we may be in danger of squelching love and compassion. We may be at risk of becoming what Beck bluntly suggested on his blog: "self-interested, callous jerks."[5] He observes that a rushed and hurried daily pattern may change us from the person we think we are or intend to be (generous, kind, loving, and compassionate) into someone morally indecisive and indifferent. If so, surely our kids will pick up on this and struggle with the contradiction—we *say* we love the Lord and our neighbors. But what do we *do?* Our actions—or inaction—may deeply impact our children's understanding of theology and resulting philosophy of life as they deal with contradictions they witnessed during hectic and harried childhoods.

Will they see us ignore not only needs in our daily path, but also the needs that come up in the news—the suffering in the world? Will they conclude what they see us conclude—that there's nothing we can do to make a difference? Instead of feeling empowered by signing up for a sponsorship program or contributing mosquito netting for malaria prevention, will they toss the paper in recycling or click away, like we do when we're in too big of a rush to consider such an opportunity to offer some compassion?

Even worse than our child witnessing our lack of compassion for others is for him to be in need of compassion himself, only to be ignored.

Hurry threatens my ability to listen and respond with compassion to my own family. Like the seminarian stepping over the victim en route to give a talk about the Good Samaritan, do I step over the needs of my children—figuratively or even literally—in order to get out the door (*Hurry!*) to a meeting or lesson, or even … a church event?

When I'm under the gun, it doesn't take much for me to sound irritable and aggravated with the children. It's hard to listen carefully and give them my full attention. In short, I'm not myself—nor am I the person I want to be—when I'm regularly overbooked and running late. A hectic schedule challenges my sensitivity to people's needs.

I don't want to rush my son's desire to slather me with good-byes. I don't want to hurry out the door when my daughter's algebra homework confounds—even if it confounds me, too (which it usually does). I want to move at a pace slow enough to notice the unusually silent ride home from school, and slow down enough to ask what happened, wait, ask again, and listen.

I want to live a slow enough life to be there for my kids. I want to be there for anyone God gives me to help. Even a stranger slumped in my path.

I can't say whether or not I would have stopped for the staged victim in the alley. I like to think I would have, even if I were in a huge hurry … but now, thinking about the seminarians, I'm not so sure.

What I have realized is that the results of the study suggest that eliminating hurry from my life will increase the odds that I'll have time and take time to help—even just to phone 911. It's compelling evidence motivating me to slow down—to be one who is more likely to serve and love.

I'm stopping and paying attention more often. I'm trying to make space and time to listen for the Holy Spirit and respond to His prompts. I'm convinced that I'm going too fast if I can't stop and serve someone in need—whether it's a stranger, neighbor, friend … or one of my own kids.

Slow Notes

After sharing the details of the Good Samaritan study with a friend of mine, she sent me this note:

> I thought about the idea of living slow enough
> to care this morning as I, with elevated blood
> pressure, rudely hurried my kids out the door
> to the eye doctor. I *hate* that.
>
> Sometimes I worry about myself, that I am
> in the habit of saying, "No, not right now" to
> their requests because I *always* feel that I'm too

busy, should be doing something else, gotta use
this little piece of time while I have it, and so
on. After years of this pattern, it's getting more
and more difficult to relax and enjoy them. Of
course I'm there for the big needs and the education and if they really need to talk, but I have a
very hard time just hanging around with them.
I think that hurry can be a habit, and once
formed, it's more comfortable than downtime.

That makes me sad.

Is hurry a habit that's hurting your family? Are you more comfortable rushing your kids out the door than just hanging around
with them? Can you just relax and enjoy them?

Where's that journal?

- Make a list of things you would enjoy doing with your kids if you
  weren't in such a hurry.
- List times when you could have shown compassion and care but
  passed by because of hurry.
- Do you think your kids have a high level of compassion? Why or
  why not?
- Read aloud the story of the Good Samaritan. Discuss it and be
  vulnerable as you explore how much or little you've done to help
  others in need. Take notes in the journal.
- Apologize for times you've stepped over their needs and ignored
  their cries for compassion.

- Together, resolve to find ways to help others in everyday situations. Generate a list.
- Hold the door for several people at the post office.
- Perform an anonymous act of kindness for someone who seems flustered and rushed.
- Let someone take the better parking space.
- Choose the longer line at the grocery store and smile at the clerk.
- Start practicing a slower life yourself and as a family ... then start passing on its benefits to others who are struggling with hurry.

Live from the Slow Zone: *Lynn House*

My husband has MS, and when he's relaxing with friends watching TV, or even at work where he sits a lot, his symptoms aren't obvious. But the reality is that he gets fatigued and weak very quickly. We're trying to get our house ready to sell, but it's hard for him to get much done, and I can't do it alone. So I sent out an email plea to some close friends explaining the situation and asking if they could help. Everyone responded with great encouragement, but two made a huge impact on me.

One friend called in tears, so touched to finally get a real glimpse into our struggles. Her family had been intending to serve a missionary family and give them a break, but the details weren't coming together. When she got my email, she knew God was telling her that this was why—that their family was to be helping us here at our home. So her family showed up over Christmas break, and they cleaned out the entire basement. They helped me pack up toys, move furniture, fill Goodwill bags, organize Christmas decorations, and change lightbulbs. She said that it hit her how we, as the body of Christ, are too busy to notice when our brothers and sisters need help, let alone find a significant amount of time to serve one another.

Another friend responded by saying that after we dropped off our kids at school, she would hop in my car and ride home with me so that she could work the entire time our kids were in school. She and her husband have one car, so she often rides the city bus; therefore, she has made it a way of life to simplify and slow down. In fact, she has simplified so much that she was able to dedicate nearly every day in January to riding home with me and attacking any chore I gave her. Talk about margins! I am truly amazed.

7 Too Fast to Rest

Sleep is a common casualty of the fast-paced family. Sustained and excessive speeds often shortchange sleep necessary to restore bodies, minds, and souls. But living underrested jeopardizes our health, leaving us susceptible to a wide variety of stress issues.

An article in *New York Magazine* about children and sleep stated that overstimulated, overscheduled kids are getting at least an hour's less sleep than they really need, "a deficiency that ... has the power to set their cognitive abilities back years."[1]

The article offered strong scientific arguments for a slower-paced life that embraces a rhythm that includes rest. For example, it appears that children's brains are a work in progress until age twenty-one. Research suggests that much of that "work" is done while a child is sleeping, and any lost sleep time appears to have an exponential impact on children that doesn't exist with adults.

One of my daughters was a sixth-grader at the time that I read that article, so this leaped off the page: "A slightly sleepy sixth-grader will perform in class like a mere fourth-grader."[2] *Two grades* lower? Well, I have to admit that when I pick up my daughter after a "sleep"-over, she seems dazed and glazed, unable to focus or stay engaged in conversation.

Zealous parents want their kids to excel, sometimes forcing them to sacrifice their sleep to complete homework assignments or to compete in certain activities, teams, and performances. But what if our earnest desire to see them excel backfires because they aren't getting the rest they need? Parents pushing their kids to develop sharp minds may pause for thought when they learn that sleep disorders can impair their child's IQ as much as lead exposure. And some studies reveal that grades go down in proportion to the minutes of sleep high school students are deprived. "Teens who received A's," the article reported, "averaged about fifteen more minutes sleep than the B students, who in turn averaged eleven more minutes than the C's, and the C's had ten more minutes than the D's.... Every fifteen minutes counts."[3]

In response to these kinds of findings, schools have attempted to experiment with a later start time in the morning. In a Minneapolis suburb, a high school changed its start time from 7:25 to 8:30 a.m. They compared math and verbal SAT scores for the top 10 percent of students. In the year preceding the time change, those scores averaged 1288; a year later, they averaged 1500, "an increase that couldn't be attributed to any other variable," the article stated.[4]

Another startling example comes from a school in Lexington, Kentucky, which also changed its start time to an hour later. "After the time change, teenage car accidents in Lexington were down 16 percent. The rest of the state showed a 9 percent rise."[5]

Evidently a good night's sleep keeps us alive and healthy in more ways than one. Families will be more alert and ready to work and study and think. Findings like these remind us that regular rest brings clarity to decision-making. Rested families might be able to enjoy less-hurried mornings as well.

But the temptation persists to pack kids' daily routines full of lessons, practices, games, and honors classes. To fit it all in, something must be given up. Can we let go of the science project? No, that's a must. How about early-morning swim practices? The chess club? The Mandarin Chinese course? The school play? Everything seems so critical that rather than drop something from the schedule, the solution is often to cheat on sleep. Parents worry that if their children give something up, it might be the one thing that would guarantee future success, the ticket to Harvard, the discovery of a hidden talent.

We must tell ourselves: *You don't have to do it all.*

And: *You must sleep.*

Another reason we cheat ourselves and our kids on sleep may be that we're haunted and dogged by the Puritan work ethic and warnings from proverbs like, "A little sleep, a little slumber, a little folding of the hands to rest—and poverty will come on you like a bandit and scarcity like an armed man" (Prov. 6:10–11; 24:33–34).

With such dire warnings ringing in our ears, we're driven to pack more than ever into twenty-four hours. And we can! The lightbulb, continuous cable, and Internet access, along with such conveniences as twenty-four-hour groceries and banking, all contribute to making it not only possible to be productive well past midnight, but they also make it seem normal to do so.

I wonder, as the National Sleep Foundation tosses out sobering statistics of car accidents attributed to sleep-deprived drivers or sluggish workers turning in sloppy work on the job, if we'll reevaluate our need for sleep. I'm not saying we need to lollygag in bed until noon, but perhaps we'll learn to stop cheating our bodies and to be good caretakers of this temple of God. Perhaps we'll fall into the rhythm built into our bodies that so obviously need regular sleep.

Go to bed on time tonight, my friend. Try to get some sleep.

Rest Is History

Just as sleep is biologically necessary, rest is spiritually essential.

Sabbath resting reminds us to rest in the Lord. Resting reminds us that the Lord is in control; that we lie down and wake up according to His will. "I lay down and slept; I awoke, for the LORD sustains me" (Ps. 3:5 NASB).

An overzealous work ethic threatens rest, as does the American obsession with entertainment, fun, and the relentless pursuit of leisure. Weekend after weekend, we speed off to destinations in search of fun-filled experiences. We refuse the rest that God has given us. We could spend time with the Lord and teach our children to do the same, learning how to read and pray together, returning to the workweek refreshed and filled, able to pour ourselves out to each other and the tasks and people who will need us. Instead, we often cram it full and return home exhausted.

In his book *The Rest of God*, Mark Buchanan contrasts the fatigue of weekend revelry with the refreshment of Sabbath keeping:

> Sanctifying some time adds richness to all time,
> just as an hour with the one you love brings
> light and levity to the hours that follow. To
> spend time with the object of your desire is to
> emerge, not sullen and peevish, but elated and
> refreshed. You come away filled, not depleted.[6]

He suggests that a wise Sabbath liturgy is, like the wise person practices in Proverbs, to consider our thoughts and attitudes and ways. He suggests that we ask ourselves, "Does the path I'm walking lead to a place I want to go? If I keep heading this way, will I like where I arrive?"[7]

It takes time to reflect on those questions. If we rush through life without a break—whether for work or play—when can we consider our ways? When can we ponder our path? We think hurry is going to get us someplace fast, when in reality, most of the time it gets us nowhere fast. Hurry inhibits the kind of healthy, wise reflection that gives us clear direction.

While we do realize some facets of God when we are in a kind of motion (when we're serving Him, practicing hospitality), Buchanan pointed out that other facets of God are discovered only through stillness.

In Exodus 14:13–14, when the Israelites stood at the Red Sea and the Egyptians were closing in on them, Moses told the people, "Do not be afraid. Stand firm and you will see the deliverance the LORD will bring you today. The Egyptians you see today you will never see again. The LORD will fight for you; you need only to *be still*." They did nothing in their own strength to escape. They didn't fight the Egyptians or run away. They needed only to be still, and God did it all. They witnessed and experienced God's strength and power as He parted the waters; by standing there doing nothing, they could attribute their deliverance to nothing and no one else.

And God made it clear that He gave us the Sabbath, a day of rest; that's why on the sixth day He gave the Israelites bread for two days. "'Everyone is to stay where he is on the seventh day; no one is to go out.' So the people rested on the seventh day" (Ex. 16:29–30). They were to be still and rest, trusting Him to provide.

It's a gift, and also a sign. The Lord said, "You must observe my Sabbaths. This will be a sign between me and you for the generations to come, so you may know that I am the LORD, who makes you holy. Observe the Sabbath, because it is holy to you" (Ex. 31:13–14).

The Sabbath is set apart and holy, a sign that points to God—it reminds us that our God is the LORD, who makes us holy.

Taking a Sabbath and doing nothing reminds us to be still and let God work.

And the stillness of Sabbath sets the stage for Jesus Christ, who did all the work for us that we might rest in Him and receive the gifts of grace, salvation, and righteousness.

When we're feeling restless, tempted to earn something—whether tangible or spiritual—and need to focus on the essence of our spiritual needs, we can borrow these simple words from King David: "My soul finds rest in God alone; my salvation comes from him" (Ps. 62:1).

When we remember the Sabbath, we will find joy not in the progress we made because we squeezed every drop of productivity and opportunity out of the week; instead, we'll rejoice in the gift of Sabbath rest reminding us that our salvation and everything that we truly need is in Christ alone. However and whenever we observe the Sabbath, it's about resting in the Lord.

Slow Notes

It's a simple way to slow down, reduce stress, and stay healthy: Go to bed early and get enough sleep. But how many of us fight against a regular bedtime?

It's common knowledge that kids need bedtime routines. If your family's bedtime routine is sped-up or unpredictable, work on developing a steadier, calmer, nightly ritual with the children:

- Tuck them in at a consistent hour.
- Give them a drink of water, of course.
- Ask about their day.
- Make up a story.
- Recite a poem.
- Sing songs.
- Read a book.
- Read a kids' devotional.
- Pray.

Don't forget yourself, though. Sleep experts recommend that adults create relaxing routines that slow down their minds and bodies as they head toward their pillows:

- Avoid caffeine.
- Power down the computer and television.
- Aim for a consistent bedtime.
- Experiment for a week at a time to determine the ideal hours of sleep you need—it may be more or less than you thought.

What about a day of rest? Pull out your journal and consider your week. Do you ever take an entire day off to rest? Do you set aside one day to do basically nothing?

Whether you follow the Hebrew model and observe the

Sabbath from sundown Friday to sundown Saturday or from morning to evening on Sunday, the first day of the week, the bottom-line concept of Sabbath is about rest. We were given that pattern—a rhythm of six days' work and one day of rest—as a gift. Why turn it down?

Explore in your Slow Notes what your family's Sabbath could look like.

- How could it be set apart from the rest of the week?
- How is worship a key aspect of the day?
- What would you stop or avoid doing? List what you do now that doesn't honor God and feels like work.
- How could your Sabbath change?
- Read Isaiah 58:13–14 to your family and ask how the entire family could honor the Sabbath by not doing as each person pleases, nor going his or her own way.
- Help the kids finish homework by Saturday so that they don't have it hanging over them on Sunday.
- Could everybody pitch in to prepare food in advance, so that nobody's stuck in the kitchen? Or simply heat up planned leftovers?
- Schedule your next vacation so that you return home on Saturday instead of Sunday, to enjoy continuity of corporate worship with your local church body.
- What relaxing, noncompetitive activity could you do together that has nothing to do with school or work or striving?
- Play could offer energetic kids—and adults—a restful and restorative Sabbath. Relax and have fun!

One day a week, stay home. Unplug. Reflect. Remember who God is, and let Him remind you who—and Whose—you are.

Live from the Slow Zone: *Andrea Birch*

I'm continually probing into what Sabbath rest means for me. Another thing I'm realizing is that the Sabbath is not only a day where I physically rest, but also a day of emotional and mental rest.

Let me explain:

My date book stays closed.

I do not plan anything, look ahead into my week, or worry about the week to come.

Instead, I focus on what the day means: a resting of the body, mind, and soul.

By resting my body, I do no unnecessary work—no catch-up, no laundry, no cleaning, no organizing. I *will* cook and clean up meal preparations.

By resting my mind, I will not plan out my coming week or yield to any worries or concerns. It is a discipline to focus on this day as being one free of worries or concerns, and mainly rest.

By resting my soul, I read and meditate on Scripture and listen to worship music as well as attend church service, where I am fed spiritually for the coming week.

Now, one might ask, "Shouldn't every day be a day of soul-level rest? Isn't that why Jesus came?"

And I would say, "Yes."

Jesus did say:

Come to me, all you who are weary and burdened,
and I will give you rest. Take my yoke upon you and
learn from me, for I am gentle and humble in heart,
and you will find rest for your souls. For my yoke is
easy and my burden is light. (Matt. 11:28–30)

Every day should be an opportunity for mental and emotional rest for our souls. This is why Jesus came and reconciled the law. The Christian life is a continual Sabbath.

But what I find on the Sabbath is that a break from the "necessities" of life—like the planning and the *doing* that are a necessary part of life—really forces me to have the emotional and mental rest on the Sabbath, just as doing no unnecessary work on the Sabbath gives my body the rest it needs.[8]

8 On Pace with Jesus

Life is not a sprint.

Yet, we live in the land that values and even glorifies speed—mind-numbing, adrenaline-churning, distracting, dangerous speed. And few families can sustain that pace over the long haul. Those that try end up with indicators that it's time to slow down.

When we push our families to sustain a pace that's too fast and exceeds limits, we'll start to see signs of wear and tear.

Is that pace of life inevitable?

I don't think so ... because as I look to Christ and try to discern in Scripture *His* pace, there's something I can't help but notice.

Jesus never seemed to be in a hurry.

When I look through the Gospels, I see that He was attentive to people's needs and deliberate about His actions. He was responsive and busy, but not frantic. He was occupied, but not frazzled. He had intense moments of ministry when healing on the Sabbath, teaching and feeding the crowds, and responding to the challenges of the Pharisees. We even read about His anger with the money changers. But there's never a sense that Jesus operated in any kind of frenetic pace. He was never harried, never hectic. Jesus' actions seemed to flow from His purposeful and decisive heart, a heart that was focused on and yielded to the Father's will, obedient unto death on a cross.

His single-minded devotion to the Father resulted in Him being unrushed. People kept asking Him to teach and heal. Even when crowds pressed in all around begging for His touch, He steadily met their needs without any anxiety. He would see the crowds and simply sit down and teach them.

The fastest things He utilized for transportation were boats. One day He mounted a donkey—clearly He wasn't looking for a speedy entrance into Jerusalem for His triumphal entry. Most of the time, He just walked.

He walked beside the Sea of Galilee. He walked from city to city. And in one of His most dramatic and awe-inspiring miracles, He walked on water. The gospel writers consistently select slow verbs to describe the Lord's pace: He *left* one place and *went* to another. He *went* out of the house and *sat* by the lake, and then He *got* into a boat and *sat* in it.

But the gospel writers knew when to insert a good, solid action verb—they were bold when the situation called for that kind of clear description. For example, they wrote that news about Jesus spread *quickly*, and people *ran* to Jesus to be healed or hear His teaching. In fact, there was often a lot of rushing and running in response to Jesus and to get to Jesus. On the morning of the resurrection, Mary *ran* to the disciples to tell the good news, and Peter and John *raced* to the tomb.

But Jesus Himself? During His time on earth, the contrast between His pace and those of the people around Him drives home His slow steadiness even more.

And He also knew how to stop completely and pull away. He withdrew by boat privately to a solitary place, but before He could get there, a crowd *ran* around the lake to meet Him. He first took time to heal, speak to, and even feed the crowd, and afterward, He did eventually *go*—presumably slowly, because the Gospels give no indication of any hurrying—by Himself on a mountainside to pray. He didn't rush up the mountain; He simply *went.*

We even see Him sleep, resting in a boat in the thick of a storm that upset the disciples. He brought calm to the lake by rebuking the winds and the waves; the Lord stilled the storm.

He moved slowly enough to reach out and touch people. In Mark 8:22–26, Jesus stopped and pulled aside the blind man, healing him privately. He looked people in the eye—something that can't be done in a hurry. In the chaos of accusations when the woman caught in adultery was about to be stoned, Jesus slowed everybody down by bending down and writing on the ground with His finger. What He wrote, nobody knows. They peppered Him with questions again, but He took His time. He eventually straightened up and proposed that whoever was without sin be the one to throw the first stone. One by one, they went away.

We have a slow and steady Savior meeting up with our own frenzied selves.

Sometimes He was so slow that His pace didn't appear to be the right pace.

When Lazarus was sick, Mary and Martha sent word to Jesus. "Lord, the one you love is sick," they said (John 11:3).

When Jesus got the message, He said that the sickness wouldn't end in death. "No, it is for God's glory so that God's Son may be glorified through it" (John 11:4). He loved that family, and so one would expect Him to head straight to Bethany—quickly—and heal His friend. Why didn't He rush?

For that matter, He could simply say the word and instantly heal Lazarus long distance—a fast and joyous solution to a sorrowful situation. He had done that before for the centurion's servant, simply saying, "Go! It will be done just as you believed it would" (Matt. 8:13). The servant was healed that very hour. He also healed a Canaanite woman's daughter from a distance. He told her, "Woman, you have great faith! Your request is granted" (Matt. 15:28). And wherever her daughter was, she was healed.

But with Lazarus, He chose not to heal instantly across time and space. Nor did He rush to their house. Instead, He waited. He stayed where He was two more days after hearing that Lazarus was sick. Then He told His disciples they would all head back, because Lazarus was dead. He was so slow in coming that by the time He arrived, Lazarus had already been in the tomb for four days. When Jesus told them to take away the stone, Martha gently pointed out that "by this time there is a bad odor, for he has been there four days" (John 11:39).

They were about to see the glory of God. A man who was so dead that decay had surely set in would be brought to life, resurrected by the slow-moving Savior. Jesus' slow pace had a long-range view rooted in His Father's divine purpose. He knew the perfect pace. His slowness glorified God. We may wonder why He tarries, but we can trust His timing in our lives. "He hath made every thing beautiful *in his time*" (Eccl. 3:11 KJV).

Is it possible to imitate the slow, steady, determined pace of the Lord? Jesus Himself thought so when He said, "Take my yoke upon you and learn from me, for I am gentle and humble in heart, and you will find rest for your souls. For my yoke is easy and my burden is light" (Matt. 11:29–30).

When animals such as oxen are yoked to one another, they must walk in tandem. They walk as one. Neither animal can forge ahead, because the two are linked to each other. Often a less mature, inexperienced animal is yoked to one that is stronger and more experienced. The experienced one sets the pace. When we yoke ourselves to Jesus, we learn from Him, from His gentle and humble heart. We walk with Him at His pace; yoked to our leader, we find rest for our souls.

If you want to follow someone, you can't go faster than the one who is leading; following Jesus cannot be done at a sprint if He is moving slowly. Jesus invited His disciples to follow Him, and they did. They walked. At *His* pace.

We can too.

Today, if we claim to live in Him, we must *walk* as Jesus did (1 John 2:6).

Slow Notes

"Be still, and know that I am God."

You've probably heard the reference from Psalm 46:10, but take time to read all of Psalm 46. You'll see that the well-known verse marks a shift in the psalm, as God's voice breaks through. In context, it's a powerful command from the Lord Himself.

As frenzied families squeeze every last bit of productivity out of the day, our minds are as full as our schedules. In the clamor of our many thoughts, there is often no room for God. We're as busy as Bethlehem, where there was no room in the inn, no room for Christ Jesus.

We're hungry for stillness.

We're craving calm.

We're starved for solitude.

When a great storm arose at sea, Jesus rebuked the wind and said, "Peace, be still" (Mark 4:39 KJV). He commanded it, and the winds obeyed immediately. Will we let our souls be stilled as well?

Many English translations use the phrase "Be still," but take note of the New American Standard, which chooses a different phrase: "*Cease striving* and know that I am God" (Ps. 46:10 NASB).

Cease striving. Acknowledge God's sovereignty. Recognize His power in your life. Stop trying to make it all happen on your own. Motivated by worry and scrambling to ensure our success (or the illusion of success), we push and strive.

For the next fifteen minutes, stop. Think about Jesus' speed.

Slow down. Be still. *Cease striving.*

Pray.

And even though the idea of walking with Christ is figurative, plan a nice, long walk by yourself or with your family today or tomorrow.

Don't treat this as a workout with hand weights and a pedometer. Just go out there and walk steadily, thinking about what it really means for you to walk with Christ.

If you're alone, pray; if you're with your child, talk with him and pray as you feel led.

When you get back, write about the experience. What did you hear, see, smell, or think?

Live from the Slow Zone: *Susan Clark*

When we were living in Belgium, I would walk Kelsea to school, which was operating on Belgian time, so school didn't start on time. The moms would stand around and talk, the kids would play, and finally when the teachers were ready, they'd call the kids in. Nobody was looking at their watch—even the moms who were on their way to work seemed unrushed and relaxed. I just got the feeling that people had more time than they do here.

There was a butcher in Leuven who opened a little restaurant and served the best steaks we've ever had. The restaurant was narrow and had maybe eight tables in it, and the owner would come out and talk with the customers, hanging out and enjoying himself. There would always be a two-hour wait to get in because everybody knew the food was so good. But we'd all wait. We'd just put in our name and walk around town.

During the month of August, most stores close down in Belgium, and people go on vacation for the entire month. Well, the guy shut down the restaurant along with everyone else. We couldn't believe it—what a contrast to America! In the States, this guy would be buying out the neighbors' buildings, knocking out walls, adding space and staff to serve more people and make more money. He never did.

We went back years later to visit, and he was still there. Everything was exactly the same. He came out and talked with us just like before. This guy's life was so simple. He was only open for a few hours in the evening. He served steak, talked with people, maybe drank a little wine, and went to bed. It was so great. It epitomized what we loved about life in Belgium. Nobody seemed to be out to make more than they needed to live off of. It's a great illustration for how life can be. Even now, all these years later and back in the States, I look at my life and see that I've moved away from that. I find myself getting caught up in our culture. It's so easy to start equating output with quality of life—but I think it's the opposite. I'm reminded to enjoy the small and simple moments.

Just the other day, my daughter Lily and I went into a toy store that we'd never been to before to shop for a birthday present. The store is wonderfully laid out with lots of color and fun things mounted up high on the ceiling. Lily walked in and gasped, "Mom! It's just like *Mr. Magorium's Wonder Emporium!*" That movie is about a magical toy store, and she felt like she had just stepped into it. She was amazed and wanted to look at everything, but I was in a hurry. I was focused on my task, and the store didn't have what we wanted, so I was ready to move on. And it's so sad, because there I was with my sweet ten-year-old daughter, who was in awe, and I was saying, "No, don't touch that. Come on. We've got to go."

I was in a hurry thinking we had to get ready for church, so I rushed her through. But we actually had enough time. We could have stayed, but I lost that moment, that newness. We can go back to that store later, but it'll never have that feeling again. It'll never again be Mr. Magorium's Wonder Emporium.

It makes me grateful for the times we *have* taken advantage of those moments of newness. One morning when we lived in Belgium, we went for a little walk and took time to feed some chickens at a farm down the road. I'm so glad we did that, because to this day, years later, my children still talk about feeding the chickens and how fun it was.

9 Too Fast to Pray or Worship

My friend Susan Clark comes from a big family that gathers for almost every birthday and holiday—even vacations. They often camp together in the Great Smoky Mountains. The year that their beloved grandmother passed away was especially precious, because Granny loved the mountains and had introduced them to camping. On that trip, they missed her presence and shared memories of her around the campfire, nodding, laughing, and then crying in turns. The slow process of grieving was rich with stories, love, and healing.

One evening they took a short hike together, and near sunset emerged at the edge of the forest overlooking a sky streaked brilliant orange. Silent, in awe, they leaned against each other, draping an arm over a shoulder or clasping hands. The colors shifted and softened from orange to subtle shades of rose.

One of the sisters began to sing.

"O Lord, my God, when I in awesome wonder, consider all the worlds Thy hands have made ... "

The rest joined in, adding layers of harmony. "I see the stars, I hear the rolling thunder, Thy power throughout the universe displayed ..."

Together they sang the chorus as tears, glistening joy, slid down their cheeks.

This is exactly what Granny did—she broke out in spontaneous song in response to awe-inspiring moments. She worshipped her great, powerful, almighty God:

> Then sings my soul, my Savior God, to Thee,
> How great Thou art, how great Thou art.
> Then sings my soul, my Savior God, to Thee,
> How great Thou art, how great Thou art![1]

What a tribute to their grandmother, and what a heritage she passed along from her children and grandchildren to her great-grandchildren—a legacy of worship. Her influence stretches beyond their family to people like me, a family friend, learning about spontaneous worship because Granny taught them to pause and glorify God and praise Him for the beauty and power of creation. I am learning a little better from their family culture how to slow down enough to worship.

As a child, I entered a slower world when I visited my own grandmother for a week in the summertime. I got a glimpse of her reverence at night. I would get ready for bed first, slip under the cool sheets, lie back on a pillow in the darkened guest room, and listen for her to finish her evening tasks and ablutions. I would crack open the door that separated our rooms just a smidge.

I heard her flip the light switch and then saw her kneel next to her bed in the shadows. Kneeling couldn't have been easy; she was nearly eighty years old at the time. Still, she knelt, every night. Through that sliver of space where the door stood ajar in the soft summer darkness, I heard her whispering.

At first, I didn't know what she was doing. Later, when I realized she was saying her prayers, I was curious, squirming across the mattress to shift close and listen in through the door. I wanted to know how she prayed and what she said, but I could never quite make it out. I'd hear a name now and then of one of my cousins, or an uncle, but most of it was soft, low, and private. Each night, I tried to find a way to hear better, but I never made out more than the gentle murmur of a beloved soul communing with her Creator.

Although I never learned details—I was too embarrassed to ask and admit that I was listening in—I fell asleep comforted and impressed that every single night my grandmother physically lowered herself to take her requests to the Lord. My grandmother modeled reverence and humility. She paused at the end of the day to worship through prayer.

Fast-paced, micromanaged families can get consumed with what's next on their pressured schedules; they need to look up now and then, to recognize who God is and who they are in light of His grandeur. We all benefit from an expression of praise and a habit of prayer—at night kneeling by the side of the bed, perhaps, or in the early morning sitting silently on the porch.

To be clear, God invites us into a relationship with Him that does not *require* us to sit still to interact with Him. We can talk with Him continuously throughout the day, wherever we are and whatever we're doing. It's a joy, grace, and privilege to talk with our Lord anytime, anyplace. He's accessible. He's gracious. When we can't slow down to worship His majesty in song or kneel and acknowledge His authority in prayer, He's not surprised. He knows our going out and our coming in and is intimately acquainted with all our sped-up ways. He knows every hair on our heads and every appointment in our iPhones. He's not surprised by our busy, hurry, and overload. He knows. He may prefer that we offer Him more of our attention and time, but He knows what we're about.

In fact, when I'm unable to stop to pray, I think of the call to "pray continually" (1 Thess. 5:17). Praying as I go is a way to weave an awareness of the Lord into every activity I undertake. I might sing something with my kids as we barrel down the road to piano lessons, reminding myself of His indwelling Spirit. While waiting in the carpool line at school for the older girls, my youngest would launch into the doxology or a simple tune he learned at church that repeats the line, "Be still and know that He is God." In the car, on the run, we seek to be internally still enough to recognize that He is God. Even simple children's songs learned at VBS and sung by our average voices can point us to profound truths, prompting prayer and thanks wherever we are. In those moments, we lift our eyes from the screens and dashboards of our daily lives and get perspective; we remember who we are, to Whom we belong, and how great He truly is.

Praise, worship, prayer, thanksgiving—these can be done on the fly, and the Lord hears us. He is Emmanuel, God with us. He is not distant or detached. Regardless of our speed, He invites communication and relationship.

He even gives us human terms to help us grasp nuances of our relationship with Him—we're His children, and He is our Father; Jesus is our Brother; He is Lord, Savior, and King, as well as Teacher, Friend, and Family:

"Who is my mother, and who are my brothers?" Pointing to
his disciples, he said, "Here are my mother and my brothers.
For whoever does the will of my Father in heaven is my
brother and sister and mother." (Matt. 12:48–50)

We are granted intimate relationship with the Lord.

But intimate relationships generally don't flourish without some dedicated time one-on-one. They need slow moments of focus and attention.

So there are also times when we stop completely in order to pray and praise.

At dinner, we pause to say grace. Our son, Daniel, loves to do the honors. He says, "thank you" over and over for specific things that God has given us and the ways He's answered prayer. He offers a long list of requests and concerns, earnestly pouring out his heart to the Lord as we hold hands and let him lead us in heartfelt prayer. By the time he's done praying, the rice might be cold, but it's worth it to hear gratitude bubble up and overflow with such sincerity and purity of heart. We humbly bow and let our little child lead us in expressing thanks.

At bedtime, we may pray or sing after listening to the concerns of each child. As the hallway light leaks into their bedrooms, I can see expressions on their dimly lit faces that I don't see in the flurry of the day; I witness restful, peaceful, thoughtful human beings beginning to rest their minds, hearts, souls, and bodies. These tender moments are sometimes rushed because we stay up too late. I hate that. But when we take our time, slow down, and linger—when we punctuate our day with a prayer—we settle into the reality that our lives are in His hands.

Our Lord deserves that faithful one-on-one time. He won't demand it; it's our choice. But during times set apart from our hectic activities, we can really pour out our hearts to Him as He listens to every joy and pain (Ps. 62:8); then we in turn take time to listen to Him as He speaks through His Word, answering prayer, granting wisdom, expecting obedience.

If we can't slow down to develop that relationship with the living God who invites us to something deeper and richer, we're going too fast. If we don't bother to pray, worship, give thanks, or stand in hushed awe at something He has created or done, we're going too fast.

In Matthew 17:1–5, Jesus took Peter, James, and John to a high mountain and was transfigured before them. Moses and Elijah appeared and talked with Jesus. And Peter spoke up, suggesting that he might build three shelters, one for Jesus, one for Moses, and one for Elijah. While he was still speaking, a bright cloud enveloped them—Peter was interrupted by God Himself, as a voice from the clouds said, "This is my Son, whom I love; with him I am well pleased. Listen to him!" (Matt. 17:5).

Upon seeing the Lord in His glory, Peter's first thought was to *talk* and to *do* something. But the voice said simply to *listen* to Jesus.

Don't *build* anything; don't *do* anything—oh, and by the way, stop talking, too.

Just … listen.

Listen to Jesus.

We need to slow down enough at all times to listen to Him. If we aren't doing that—if we can't hear His voice—we're going too fast.

Jesus says that we're to listen for His voice, the voice of the Good Shepherd. In John 10:2–4, Jesus says that the Shepherd calls His own sheep by name and leads them out; they follow Him because they *know His voice.*

Can we recognize Jesus' voice speaking to us when our heads are full of noise and our bodies are in motion? Can we hear Him when we haven't taken the time and space to slow down and listen?

Take inspiration from Susan's granny, who taught her family to stop everything, take in creation's beauty, and respond by worshipping the Creator. Let's learn to do the same, worshipping the Lord through song, poetry, recitation of Scripture, and prayers of praise.

Allow time for a habit of prayer that connects you and your family with the Lord throughout the day. Clasp hands around the table at each meal you share, recognizing our generous Provider. Kneel at bedtime in a posture of humility before a holy God and encourage children to do the same. Habits are healthy for fast-paced families. Far from becoming meaningless motions, habits of prayer reserve space in our schedules to turn to the Lord.

And while kneeling isn't necessary to prayer, it can serve as a physical reminder of our dependency. Whether we kneel or not, we come broken, spiritually poor, and needy, seeking to be heard and to be filled as we humbly bring our requests before Him.

We needn't grovel, though, because our High Priest, Jesus, makes it possible to approach the throne of grace with confidence, to receive mercy and find grace to help us in our time of need (Heb. 4:14–16). The Holy Spirit helps us in our weakness, interceding for us (Rom. 8:26–27).

Attentive communication with the living God is the foundation of meaningful relationship. Pay attention and pray while in motion—but slow down as well to commune intimately with the lover of our souls.

Like Samuel, we can ask to hear His voice:

"Speak, for your servant is listening" (1 Sam. 3:10).

Slow Notes

One avenue to more meaningful connection with the Lord is through His Word. First, we have to slow down enough to actually sit down and do it. Then we need to ask the Holy Spirit to speak to us. And then we have to slow down enough to engage with the text.

There are many ways to do this. I collected several quiet time/devotional ideas and posted them online at www.NotSoFastBook.com, but I thought I'd highlight one in particular that is delightfully slow.

Two young men came to our Sunday-morning class to talk about their devotions. They've been *writing out* the Scriptures, word for word, starting with Genesis.

They call it "scribing," a way to slow down and engage with every single word, not glossing over a jot or tittle. My friend Lucia is also "scribing" the New Testament, starting with Matthew. All of the "scribes" reported that the Word is coming to life for them. They inspired me to copy Mark, and I agree. Because "all Scripture is God-breathed" (2 Tim. 3:16) and has been preserved for us over millennia, writing out a passage honors that truth. It's a way to say, "If all Scripture is God-breathed, I don't want to miss one word."

Want to try scribing? The young men invested in beautiful leather journals for their project, whereas Lucia and I bought inexpensive composition books on sale. High-end or humble, you, too, can handwrite Scripture to connect with every word. And for kids, it develops attentiveness while serving as handwriting practice.

Start with a superfamiliar passage such as Psalm 23. Writing each word helps bring it to life in a fresh, new way; plus, that psalm contains powerful visuals of a not-so-fast life. As you write, ponder what green pastures and still waters could do for your family.

Live from the Slow Zone: *Sharon Stohler*

There are plenty of days when I'm bored at home. I float around from room to room, looking at all the scuff marks on the walls and the crumbs on the floor. I *could* clean that up—again—but I'd rather not. I ask my husband to paint the walls because I get so tired of looking at the same color day in and day out. Even the conversation at dinner seems dull. "Well … we did math and then grammar, and then some history. Same old, same old." Nobody phoned. Nobody stopped by. There were no fascinating people to meet or water-cooler conversations to ponder. Nobody to chat with about the latest new fashions. Just my kids and me, homeschooling, day after day, 180 days a year.

I guess this may sound rather bleak, and you might be wondering why in the world I would choose this lifestyle. Well, there are many wonderful reasons, but there is one major reason: The pace of this life allows me to hear God's voice. That voice—*His* voice—is way more important to my growth and the overall health of my family than any tip on new jeans or reality television I might receive.

Since I'm not scrambling to get out the door each day, I can take the time to sit with the Lord and listen to what He has to say to me. I can talk with Him throughout the day as I run the dust rag over the furniture, rather than run from one activity to the next. When He challenged my husband to enter into full-time ministry, I was able to hear Him clearly, because I was quiet. His voice led me to continue home education. His whisper caused me to consider adopting an African orphan boy, which we did. I believe these instances were a direct result of my home-based, slow-paced, simple life.

It's allowed me to still the noise and hear the whisper.

10 Load Limits

In the late 1800s, Englishman Samuel Plimsoll documented evidence that each year nearly a thousand sailors were drowning on ships around British shores as a result of overloading. Disturbed and determined, he took up a crusade to reform the British shipping industry. To ensure the safety of both crew and cargo, Plimsoll argued that ships must sail at capacity or lighter.

Every ship has a different capacity for cargo—that is, every ship has limits; therefore, Plimsoll promoted a plan requiring vessels to bear a standardized, permanent mark called a "load line" that would indicate when it was overloaded.

After determining a ship's limit, the load line would be permanently fixed on the vessel amidships on both sides of the hull. If the mark dipped below the waterline during loading, something would have to be removed or else the ship was in danger of taking on water.

Plimsoll's tireless efforts led Parliament to pass the Merchant Shipping Act into law. From that point on, a standardized mark called the Plimsoll line or Plimsoll mark (later the International Load Line)—a circle with a horizontal line running through it—was emblazoned on the side of every cargo ship to indicate its official limit.[1]

The point of this little lesson in maritime history?

When I look around, I see friends and neighbors overloaded, riding dangerously low in the water, attempting to sail treacherous waters every single day. Each one of us has limits, yet many of us push those limits daily. We've joined the world as it races to exceed all expectations, creating more and more at faster and faster rates. We seem to imagine life with no limits, which is freeing and exciting, and in the name of speed, productivity, and efficiency, we pile on more and more—risking more and more as we do. We risk our health, our families, and our faith.

But we're living in denial because in reality, we, like ships, have limits.

Dr. Richard Swenson once remarked to a friend that humans will never run a one-minute mile. The friend briefly paused and then replied, "Never say never." Swenson wrote:

> Just the fact that we are willing to even consider the possibility of a one-minute mile in itself illustrates the fact that we have a problem truly accepting our limits.... If you refuse to make the statement that we will never be able to run a one-minute mile, then let's push further. How about thirty seconds? If you still hold out, then how about five seconds?
>
> Eventually, you will have to agree that we have limits.

> The position I am taking is not always
> popular.... Many of our leaders, thinkers,
> inventors, and motivators are teaching us to
> think big, to think of all the possibilities, to
> assault the impossible. And that's good. But
> we must be careful and we must be precise,
> for ... [w]hen we start to pretend that some-
> how we don't have limits, we get ourselves
> mired in painful consequences.[2]

Self-help gurus would consider Swenson and me negative voices inhibiting potential ... and to be honest, I myself don't like hearing it. But he's right. Every human being has certain limits. Some are obvious once we start listing them: We aren't infinite, for example; we only have twenty-four hours in a day and some of those hours must be devoted to rest; and, contrary to what some clever car and cell phone commercials might suggest, we can only inhabit one place in space and time.

It's only God who has no limits.

In His infinite wisdom, however, He created us finite.

But we routinely deny this fact and load our lives to capacity, sailing off as if all is normal and safe, denying the nagging feeling that we're on the brink of going under. *Besides,* we tell ourselves, *everybody else is as weighed down as we are and seems to be managing just fine—who are we to complain or lessen our load?*

We're uneasy, but we're afloat ... pretty much.

Besides, no Plimsoll has come to our side and highlighted the danger. No one is crusading for change. Until now.

Individual Load Lines

Every person is like a ship, with a specific and limited God-determined capacity for activities and obligations unique to that individual.[3] Some can take on extremely heavy loads on a daily basis and only barely exhibit signs of stress—they thrive on challenges, complications, and chaos and might feel bored if their ship is riding light and high in the water for too long. These driven, high-achieving, high-capacity, Type A personalities know how to get things done.

They remind me of aircraft carriers, because they're at their best when there's a ton of action, with people coming and going, tasks to complete, and problems to solve. They may even enjoy a little risk or danger—if they don't do their job right, something could fall apart. These productive people run committees and corporations and shuttle their kids to multiple sports, camps, and enrichment programs without missing a beat.

Trouble is, they set the standard for others who may be able to juggle only a few responsibilities before taking on water. The world and even churches often assume that all people can handle the same hefty loads as the powerful, efficient, and productive aircraft carriers, but some people are lighter ships with shallower cargo holds. It's hard for the sailboats and fishing trawlers of the world to say no without feeling guilty, weak, or second-rate. These people feel like they're letting others down if they say no, but they can't do it all, not without consequences—even if it's as mild as developing stress acne or an annoying facial tic. They focus on a few tasks and do those well, but when they agree to too much, even the things they do well start to suffer.

Every ship is valuable for its unique purpose. But sometimes only aircraft carriers are celebrated, and few people feel free to simplify their lives in a way that reflects their limited capacities. As a result, many schooners and rowboats continue to operate as if they're carriers.

We're at risk. Many of us are strained by the heavy loads we're bearing. If we want to make it over the long haul, we'd best determine those limits and monitor the stress of the ship.

To do so, we pray and seek wisdom from the Master Craftsman, the Shipwright Himself. The One who built us knows what we were made for; He knows our limits and load-bearing capacity. We can also ask the Lord to use those who know us well to provide us with input, telling us when they've seen us exceed our limits and take on water.

After several long seasons of sailing regularly overloaded—and very nearly going under—I've concluded that I'm definitely not an aircraft carrier. Nor am I a Carnival Cruise ship, as fun as it might be to continually entertain friends and host parties.

I'm just a *little* boat. A tugboat, perhaps, encouraging others and pulling them along at times. Or better yet, because I love seafood, I think of myself as a shrimp boat: sturdy and hardworking, but ideally focused on one main task at a time. My default mode? Keep things simple and pared down, and do those few things well.

A couple of years ago, I thought I could handle a bigger career commitment, so I partnered with someone to start a corporate writing business. We agreed that if for any reason it wasn't working, we could dissolve the partnership and the other could go solo. The business started quite well, and within a few months, projects were rolling in. But the work, I soon found, was more than this little shrimp boat could handle.

I couldn't sustain that level of activity as my regular mode of operation without stressing out. When I tried to manage work while keeping up with family and household obligations, my nets were in knots and I was sailing in circles. *Glug, glug, glug.* I poured out my heart to the Lord one afternoon and felt that the Holy Spirit was confirming the obvious: I'd hit my limit. I was not going to survive any squalls at sea. Later that day, I made an appointment with my writing partner and told her I couldn't handle it; I needed to step out of my leadership role. Per our agreement, she graciously released me from the partnership obligations and is successfully running the business herself—she is, by the way, one of those natural aircraft carriers. In addition to her work, she serves the Lord by serving people with her boundless energy, determination, numerous gifts, and inner strength. I'm impressed with her and wish I could follow her example, but I had to face my limits. Recognizing, understanding, and accepting my personal limits was a big—if humbling—step for me personally.

Overloaded? We need to eliminate, but it's hard to let go of some responsibilities and tasks. Sometimes we believe we're the only ones who can do a certain job, or we hang on to mundane chores at home out of habit or perfectionism. If someone else can do the job 60 percent as well as I, then I can delegate: Can the kids weed the flower bed or walk the dog? Could a neighbor boy prime the siding of the shed? Could my spouse clean the bathroom, even just once in awhile?

Brainstorm creative solutions for lifting the load off of a listing ship.

The Family Load Line

Not only does each person in a family have limits, but the family unit has a load line as well.

What's the difference? The family fleet, if you will, is not determined by the sum total of each individual ship's capacity—one must take into account not only the person with the greatest capacity, but also the one with the least. Concessions must be made to accommodate those who are easily overwhelmed (if they're stretched, however, they *can* grow from it) as well as those who are used to nonstop activity (although they *can* learn to rest from time to time). Because of the personal nature of a family's load line, it's impossible to determine standard comparisons for overload. Each family must seek God's wisdom to reveal their family's standard capacity.

The family organizer—often the mom—influences the family load line, orchestrating schedules and transportation. It's easy to drag along the child assuming his capacity is the same as everyone else's, but that's not necessarily the case. Sometimes adjustments must be made to respect the entire family fleet. With flexibility and a willingness to try, families can experiment and stretch, but pushing individual family members beyond their emotional or physical limits needs to be analyzed with sensitivity and compassion. The ships must *all* stay afloat to maintain a successful fleet.

Situations and stages of life can also affect the load limit of both individuals and families. The first months after the arrival of a new child, for example, can limit capacity; everyone may hit overload much faster than before and need to adjust to stay buoyant. And a family with a special-needs child is going to have an internal load much heavier than others. But it can change for the better, too—as kids grow older, the family fleet may be able to take on more.

Accepting Limits Leads to Dependence

Accepting our limits reminds us that apart from the Lord, we can do nothing (John 15:5); apart from Him, we have no good thing (Ps. 16:2). Our limits remind us that when we rely on Him, abide in Him, we experience life and grace and power, which cannot be achieved on our own strength or with our own abilities.

Accepting our limits isn't an excuse to be lazy or mediocre. It means respecting and embracing how God has made us instead of letting the world determine our capacity. And we get to see Him at work.

Margin

If we learn our limits and remain at or above our personal and family Plimsoll mark, we have some wiggle room. We can be available to each other and to other people. It's like having more margin on a page or more trunk space in the SUV. When somebody comes to us with a need, we can make time for her. I was sitting with two new friends for coffee one morning, and one of these ladies received word by cell phone of a family crisis she was going to face when she got home.

Immediately, the other friend offered to assist in any way that she could. "Do you want to ride together, or should I follow you over there?" She had time to serve her friend during this crisis. Because she wasn't overloaded, she was available, and God used her to help her friend almost the entire day.

Extraordinary Times—Extraordinary Loads

There are times when ships are called to exceed their limits to take on extraordinary tasks.

If you'll permit another ship analogy …

During the World War II battle at Dunkirk, Allied troops in northern France and Belgium were cut off by German forces—they were trapped, with the English Channel at their backs and no place to retreat. A large-scale evacuation was ordered. A fleet of destroyers would lift men directly from the beaches, but a hastily assembled fleet of smaller, civilian vessels such as fishing boats, ferries, and pleasure crafts supplemented the mission. The call was sent out for anything that floated. In answer to that call, about seven hundred boats crossed over and carried men from the shallow waters of the beaches to the large destroyers waiting offshore, saving them from captivity or death.

The leaders hoped to save one-hundred thousand men. Instead, thanks in part to the little ships, more than three-hundred thousand soldiers were rescued from Dunkirk, France.

Small ships were called to a mighty task, an emergency lifesaving mission. Those boats were surely loaded heavier than ever before, attempting to save every possible soldier and ferry each one to safety.

Sometimes we, too, are called to an exceptional task—where the Lord asks us to do something far beyond our everyday capacity. If we're called to it, He will equip and empower us, sustaining us. When it's *His* work—not us piling it on ourselves—we have the pleasure of seeing His grace at work in us. Like the little ships of Dunkirk, we can take on far more than we normally would, for His glory, and He will be glorified through us as He exhibits His supernatural strength working in our creaky little ships.

Just as Jesus kept the little ship together during a storm on the Sea of Galilee, He is able to keep us from going under. Even if we're overloaded and our Plimsoll mark dips deep underwater, we will experience His power and sustenance in order to complete the calling. Perhaps we'll come alongside a friend who is ill and serve him in tangible, daily ways beyond what we thought we could handle. Or we'll care for our aging parents, or pitch in with a mission project where the Lord clearly wants our involvement.

It's when on a regular basis we weigh *ourselves* down that we're sailing at risk. When we attempt to accomplish it all on our own, we're endangering ourselves, our families, and all that we've committed to. Of course our dear Lord is gracious, and if we find ourselves sinking due to our own choices, He very well may undertake a rescue operation to save our own sinking ship—but why not learn to sail within our limits? When He needs us, we'll be ready—sturdy, solid, and seaworthy.

Slow Notes

Shipping News

Ships come in all shapes and sizes and serve many purposes. Here are a few notes to help your family build a fun fleet analogy. See if you can find each family member in one of these vessels.

- Aircraft Carrier: This massive, powerful warship can handle incredible weight, acting as an airbase at sea. Continuous activity such as planes and helicopters landing and taking off from the flight deck make it an intense, dangerous, but exhilarating workplace.[4]
- Cargo Ship/Freighter: Loaded with goods and often designed for a special task, cargo ships are created for hefty loads, sailing confidently across the world's oceans. They work hard without tiring out.[5]
- Barge: This flat-bottomed boat can handle heavy goods in rivers and canals, but needs a partner—a tugboat or towboat—to push or pull it along.[6]
- Tugboat: The helpful tugboat is quite strong for its size and highly maneuverable as it serves other ships. Plus, it's cute as can be in children's books![7]
- Shrimp boat: Dragging its nets for pink gold, the shrimp boat isn't afraid to get dirty as it moves slowly and steadily through shallow waters day after day to complete a specific task.[8]
- Sailboat: Sloops, cutters, and schooners are all types of sailboats with shallow limits. These pleasure vessels can be thrilling to navigate but aren't built for true cargo such as the load that a freighter would transport.[9]
- Cruise Ship: A bustling, high-energy, entertaining passenger ship, the cruise ship does more than transport people to a fun-filled destination—it *is* a fun-filled destination. People love to gather on this ship. Party on!
- Pontoon: A simple, practical, fun little craft, the simplest type of pontoon floats on lakes in the summertime atop buoyant barrels. Pack a cooler with soft drinks and relax with friends and family.

- Destroyer: A fast, maneuverable, long-endurance ship that's armed and dangerous, the destroyer escorts larger vessels and defends them against attacks from submarines and aircraft. Some carry nuclear missiles that can destroy an entire city. I hate to even ask, but does this sound like anyone you know?[10]
- Ferry: You need help getting from here to there? Take a ferry. This busy, helpful craft can handle a lot of weight and doesn't mind repetition, faithfully carrying cars, people, and/or cargo from point A to point B and back again.[11]
- Rowboat: Remember summer vacation, rowing across a lake, occasionally swinging an oar against the aluminum sides with a thunk? A rowboat can usually only carry a couple of friends and some fishing gear, but it's durable enough to serve a summer camp for decades.
- Dinghy: Who's the family dinghy? The humble, utilitarian dinghy is carried by a larger boat as a lifeboat or for excursions where docking is difficult. It's not a strong boat, but it's essential to slip in where bigger crafts can't go.[12]
- Raft: Picture Huckleberry Finn poling down the river on a raft formed from a few logs lashed together. Useful, humble, yet precarious, a raft can't handle much at all before tipping.
- Yacht: Ah, the luxury yacht. Not exactly known for hard labor, but quite busy. People love to sail with friends or family on this high-end, high-class recreational craft.[13]
- Speedboat: Fast and fun, speedboats are made to zoom across the water effortlessly at high speeds without feeling stressed. You can't pile on a load of steel and expect it to stay afloat, but with a full tank of gas it pulls friends along on skis with boundless energy.

In your journal, consider the following:

- Describe various types of people you've observed in terms of the ship analogy—do you know any aircraft carriers? Sailboats? Dinghies? Or *(gulp)* destroyers?
- Have fun building an analogy referencing and expanding on the ship descriptions. What kind of ship do you think you are?
- What's your current load?
- Is this more than your ship can handle safely on an everyday basis? If so, how could you lighten the load?
- Write about a time when you were required to take on more than you normally could handle—was it something God called you to? Were you able to experience His grace, power, and sustenance keeping you afloat?
- Ask what ship your spouse sees himself (and you) as, and then share your own observations. Together try to determine the children's capacities and come up with a picture of the family fleet. Does anything need to change as a result of appreciating each person's unique limits?
- Next family night, talk about capacity and limits. Use the Shipping News information to describe various ships.

Live from the Slow Zone: Gia Tubbs

I used to spin too many plates. There was always so much going on, and I was absolutely dead tired and completely stressed.

When I first heard the ship analogy, I was unsure what kind

of boat I was. My husband thought I was like a tugboat, taking on everybody else's stuff. But sometimes I felt I was a tugboat in high gear, running like a speedboat. When life got too chaotic or I had to deal with too many people, I felt stressed. Things weren't working, and I knew I needed to find my ideal pace and type of ship.

I value one-on-one time with my kids, so I knew I was not an aircraft carrier. Maybe I could function like one, but that's not who I really was. I decided I was probably a rowboat because I really cherish that simple, intimate time with family. But I also realized that the demands of life can change things: I might be a rowboat, but I also might have to operate like several different boats throughout the week. On a given day I just might have to operate like a speedboat!

I'm learning how to say no to things. We're living a simpler life because I've learned that I really have to focus on the things that are important to me—to get homeschooling off the ground and to be a good wife.

It all goes by so fast—life, parenting, time with family. I see so many families missing important moments, and I don't want that to happen to me. My oldest daughter is a talker and wants my full attention to listen. Sometimes I think, *I do not have time for this. Get to the point.* But I *need* to have that time. What better way could time be spent than listening to a teenaged child who wants your undivided attention? I need to not be so harried.

It all goes by too quickly—don't rush it.

11 Forget the Joneses

An acquaintance told me that his son earned a National Merit Scholarship for a perfect PSAT score.

I was impressed. "Congratulations!" I said. "You must be so proud!"

Shortly after, insecurity kicked in.

Should I rush to Borders on my way home to search for a Kaplan study guide or some kind of PSAT-prep handbook for fifth-graders? My confidence wobbled, and I was guilty of comparing our family to others and feeling that we came up short. Interactions like those tempt me to alter our parenting choices in hopes of experiencing similar success.

A few years ago, a friend told me that her daughter made the elite travel soccer team, and she later shared that the team made it to the finals of a national tournament. I congratulated her both times and said, "Wonderful! You must be so proud!" Because it is wonderful, and she should be proud, and I am happy for her!

Shortly after, however, uncertainty crept in, and I launched an anxious conversation with my spouse expressing doubt over our decision to stick with a recreational soccer league.

Neighbors, friends at church, work colleagues—they all tell stories that make me question our slow-paced life. Look at their successes! What if we're wrong? Should we speed up again and model ourselves after them?

Next thing you know, I'm comparing and contrasting—feeling good or falling short.

I'm so weak. I try to resist the lure of success, wondering, *Am I getting swept into other people's ideas of what matters most? Am I shifting toward their values?*

I want to simply celebrate with people, free from the urge to set their kids or their possessions or their work or even their faith against mine and see how we measure up. I try to be strong and content, to trust that the choices we've made are right for us, that we've been listening to the voice of God and letting Him lead us.

When his devotional book *My Utmost for His Highest* was published in 1935, Oswald Chambers couldn't have known how popular that infamous Christmas communiqué, the family newsletter, would become in the twenty-first century. But Chambers' December 29th entry suggests he was granted the foresight to know that we'd be reading lengthy reports of other families' accomplishments, acquisitions, promotions, and travelogues for the year just coming to a close … and that we might be struggling. He advised:

> Do not look at someone else and say—Well, if
> he can have those views and prosper, why can-
> not I? You have to walk in the light of the vision
> that has been given to you and not compare
> yourselves with others or judge them, that is
> between them and God. When you find that a
> point of view in which you have been delighting

> clashes with the heavenly vision and you debate,
> certain things will begin to develop in you—a
> sense of property and a sense of personal right,
> things of which Jesus Christ made nothing. He
> was always against these things as being the root
> of everything alien to Himself. "A man's life
> consisteth not in the abundance of the things
> that he possesseth."[1]

Chambers knew how quickly comparison could mess up a person's relationship with the Lord and with other people as well. I have to walk in the light of the vision that has been given to me and not compare myself or my family with others or judge them, because comparing and certainly judging helps no one. In a way, I've got to forget the proverbial Joneses in order to love whomever the real-life Joneses are in my life—new friends and old, neighbors and family members, work associates, Bible-study members, and book-club participants.

I think that looking to others for inspiration is fine—in fact, I've hoped to provide slow-down ideas by introducing you to the *Live from the Slow Zone* families. But that whole keeping up with the Joneses thing so easily jeopardizes friendship, support, and unity. Copycatting or "besting" other people's choices threatens the relationship, reducing it to superficial comparison at best and tempting cutthroat competition at worst. It squelches the compassion and empathy to which Christ calls us. It stifles love.

To steer clear of the comparison trap, we could hole ourselves up from the rest of society to avoid hearing about people's successes.

But that's no way to live. If we're a slower-paced family that's truly seeking God, we'll be a part of people's lives, continually interacting with others who have chosen a high-speed lifestyle. Besides, one of the joys of a slower-paced life is that we actually have time to talk. We have time to build relationships. Our lives are slow enough that we can actually interact with others!

By living a balanced life that respects our family's speed and load limits, we're making room for people, for relationships. I really do want to celebrate that young man's National Merit Scholarship. I truly want to share in the pride of that young woman's soccer accomplishment. Instead of comparing our family to anyone else's, I want to focus on others and their needs so that I can rejoice with those who rejoice and weep with those who weep. This is a beautiful benefit of living a slower life—it should free up time to celebrate with friends who are winning and commiserate with those who are struggling.

But while rubbing shoulders with others—with the world around me—I'll continually face temptations to rev up the minivan, merge into the fast lane again, and cruise alongside the rest of the culture. I've got to check myself—am I looking to pile on activities and return to an insane schedule just to keep up (or get ahead)?

If so, I'm going to do more harm than good to my health, my sense of self, my relationship with the Lord, my family, and the very friends I'm comparing myself with.

So I pray. I pray for my puny little self-focused heart to resist the temptation to compare. I pray I'll let go of my hankering to pack my schedule full again. I pray my motives will be revealed so I can examine them and cut them off before they wreak havoc on my family's pace of life and, more importantly, their (and my) commitment to Christ.

And while I'm at it, I pray that my heart's capacity to love and pour into people will expand.

Heavenly Father, please give me Your perspective and Your heart so that I can see my life through Your eyes—not in comparison with others. Keep me from piling on more and speeding up to look like others or race against others. Let my relationships be a joyful, healthy gift that You use to inspire our family to follow You more closely and love each other more deeply. Release me from insecurity, reminding me instead to trust and depend on You for meaning and true success. In Jesus, amen.

Slow Notes

- List the top ten people who seem to leave you in awe—those folks whose lives tempt you to pack your schedule full in order to gain the same results.
- Pray for each one.
- Write out in your own Slow Notes a list of the next steps God is directing your family to take. Describe your family's priorities and values based on Scripture passages that have led you to those conclusions.
- Next time the Christmas newsletters start rolling in, pray for the senders. And if you feel tempted to compare yourself to them, pray for yourself and return to your list, to what God is revealing about you and how He wants you to live.

Live from the Slow Zone: *Rachel Anne Ridge*

If you are the parent of a three-year-old, you may have already been asked if he or she is signed up for soccer yet. Or dance. Or gymnastics. Or whatever.

They look so cute in their little uniforms! So you sign up.

And It Begins.

It starts getting complicated when you (a) have more than one child, or (b) your child likes more than one sport, or (c) your child shows potential in their chosen sport, or (d) more than one child shows potential in one or more sports. Add to this mix the other variables of schoolwork, church, and family time, and you have a real challenge to keep all the wheels on.

One of the hardest challenges to face is when your kid is pretty good and someone leans over and suggests that he or she really should be playing "Select." The competition is so much better, and it will really prepare them for playing at the high school and college level. In fact, if your kid has any hope of playing on the high school team, you have no choice but to play Select.

Year-round.

Oh, and it's expensive.

We know parents who work second jobs and run up their credit cards so that their kids can play on Select teams. They make multiple two-hour round trips to practices (and that's just in the car) and spend every weekend at tournaments.

Multiply that by just one other sibling, and they are almost never home.

Statistics will tell you that only a very tiny percentage of kids will ever play sports in college and even fewer will make it to the professional level. If you are thinking that you are investing in your child's education by funding expensive sports leagues, think again. There are far more scholarships available to good students who are good citizens than to athletes. So what is a parent to do? Well, here is what we have done, if it helps.

- We generally limit sports to one per year, per kid. We did consider two sports for one of our kids, but the seasons overlapped and we decided against it. We don't go from baseball to soccer to hockey, and it just works for us. Every kid needs time off, even from something they love.
- The girls took music lessons in addition to a sport, so for the sport season it was crazy at times. We were okay with that, because it didn't last long. After a few seasons, they weren't all that interested in sports, and we let it go.
- We have not done Select teams. We aren't against them by any means, but we can't afford the time or the money. We have done the recreation leagues and the school leagues and may consider a Select team in the future if my husband can coach. Coaching would give us a discount and would give our son and him time together. Many factors must fall into place for it to work.
- No one gets to sign up for anything before we discuss it thoroughly. (This goes for any activity, not just sports.)

To live simply you have to start by taking a hard look at your time, money, and resources and choose to live within them. By limiting our involvement in sports, we have freed up time to do other things: homework, hanging out, fishing, and not eating every meal out of a bag in the car.

Making choices about our family's activities is an ongoing process. It changes with each new sport season, school year, and event. We've often found ourselves in over our heads (particularly in December and May), going way too many directions. And that's with the best of intentions! Passing kids off like batons as you race from one thing to another is no way to live, and not what I want my kids to remember of their childhood.

We want sports to be part of our lives, not to rule our lives.[2]

12 Slow Enough to Savor Traditions

Before he retired, my dad worked odd hours as a news editor. He often went into work in the afternoon and came home at one or two in the morning after getting the paper out. I have vivid childhood memories of rare occasions during the summer when Mom would let my brother and me stay up (or nap on the couch) until Dad came home. On those special nights, Dad would stop at the only fast-food restaurant open at that time of night: White Castle. Oh yeah, baby, he'd bring home a bag of sliders, and we'd all sit at the dining room table passing around the little cardboard boxes and munching those smelly, greasy square burgers.

Man! That was the good life! White Castle at two in the morning—and I wasn't even a college student!

My parents stumbled into a tradition that formed a memory I've carried with me for decades.

But it wasn't about White Castle—it was the fact that my dad was thinking of us on his way home, and we were thinking about him as we stayed up late. And when the White Castle and Dad arrived, we were all together—albeit at an odd time of day—but that's what worked because of our family's unusual schedule.

Families can carry on traditions that represent and honor a long heritage tracing down through one's roots—African dances, Irish blessings, Jewish holidays, Chinese New Years—or they may stumble into something unwittingly and serendipitously, like our late-night White Castle. But whether they're unique to your family or tied in with centuries of cultural meaning, traditions can help families develop a group identity.

My friend Marilyn described birthdays at their house, where they go around the table and share one thing about the birthday boy or girl—one thing they admire or want to acknowledge. It could be as simple as, "I love that you always play with me," or something more substantial about the person's character. This tradition has the purpose of building each family member up through meaningful, honest words of blessing. Marilyn's daughter said she recalled one birthday when her brother applauded her purity, knowing it was a commitment she'd made and kept that hadn't always been easy.

My family thrives on traditions—we camp in Florida almost every year, have an involved Advent countdown and devotional time at Christmas, eat crepes once a week, let the birthday person pick the food for the entire day, spend New Year's Eve with friends, and watch the Super Bowl with a particular family. My family also cleans the house together once a week. This tradition isn't necessarily a warm and fun family event we look forward to with joy like a family game night, but it does pull us together toward a unified goal with measurable results. We pitch in as a team to get it done and often invite someone over the next day, practicing hospitality that's possible as a direct result of this regular tradition of shared work.

Traditions that happen with some kind of regularity, like Marilyn's family birthday blessings, build anticipation while grounding us; they add stability and meaning while injecting rhythm into our schedules. Traditions like that slow us. They provide checkpoints where we can sit down and pause for a moment, enjoying the predictable and finding reassurance in relationships. They create memories and communicate love. Traditions say, "This is who we are as a family. This is what we do together every night at bedtime, every Sunday afternoon, or each and every Christmas Eve."

You could even make traditions out of simple, loving rituals like snuggle times, group hugs, good-bye kisses, notes tucked into a sock drawer or lunch box, and hearts drawn with lipstick on the bathroom mirror (one for each person in the family). These small gestures offer everyday significance to moments otherwise lost to routine.

Yet even routines can turn into a kind of tradition, adding repetition that reassures kids that their family unit is healthy and will stick together: Washing dishes together, serving Sunday ice cream sundaes, or even the act of saying or singing grace before meals are simple but powerful routines-turned-traditions.

Shared interests can unite families and build memories. Some friends of ours love skiing together—their experiences on the slopes over the years have become a huge part of their winter memories. Another family we know loves community theater; I remember that one fall all of them, youngest to oldest, got involved in the musical *Annie,* whether as an actor or behind the scenes as stage crew. Yet another family shares a passion for music—they sing together and play instruments as a normal part of their family life.

Sometimes children mark time and seasons more by traditions than by the turning of a calendar page. They know Friday nights include the traditional movie and popcorn; Saturday mornings mean Mickey Mouse pancakes, while Sundays are for roast beef and rest. Some kids may think of Christmas starting with an Advent wreath and candlelight countdown; New Year's is watching the ball drop while munching tortilla chips and queso dip; Valentine's Day is a family love feast with red Jell-O and homemade love notes; the Fourth of July is a parade and cookout; August is an end-of-summer backyard campout; November is a Thanksgiving feast with thankful notes penned to family and friends.

Several years ago, I took note of what author and counselor Mary Pipher wrote: "When adults are surveyed about what they remember most fondly from their childhoods, most fondly recall time outdoors, holidays and vacations."[1] We've kept those three elements in mind—outdoors, holidays, and vacations—and every once in awhile, a successful camping trip will pull them all together.

Over time, some traditions can get stale or forced, so it's okay to let go of or reinvent an event, menu, or outing if it just isn't working—families will evolve to where a little-kid tradition no longer fits the teenagers those little kids have become. Then it's fine to retire the old tradition and let it reside in family memories. You could introduce a completely new tradition or adapt a favorite activity for the older set.

And sometimes too many traditions can end up meaningless when packed in with everything else—a too-full, too-fast life breezes past these sweet moments of connecting.

Our family tries to stay flexible. We experiment and adapt. We retire what no longer works and celebrate when we stumble into something new that "fits" us. Whether the tradition is new or old, however, we try to slow down enough to enjoy it—and let the tradition slow us down as well.

As you experiment with your own family traditions, be careful not to feel pressured to pile too much onto the schedule. Make it easy on yourself and keep it uncomplicated—sometimes the easiest, cheapest, least time-consuming ideas make the most meaningful memories. After all, as my own childhood memory can attest, warm moments of family togetherness can be as simple as bringing home a bag of White Castle and sharing it around the table late at night. Together.

Slow Notes

Identify your own family's "slow" traditions. Do you already enjoy ...

- Saturday-morning pancakes?
- Group hugs?
- Fall camping trips?
- Candlelit dinners?
- After-dinner walks?
- Family read-alouds?
- Touch football games?

If you don't currently have any healthy family traditions, incorporate something new over the next few weeks that fits into life (without adding logistical burdens), and ask the kids:

- *What activities are most important to you … and why?* Sometimes we think we know what they love most; we might be surprised at the answer.
- *What would you be willing to give up in order to spend more time together as a family?* You may find that they won't need or even want to do all that they're doing, and if you can let go, they might be more than happy to do so. Or maybe they prefer to continue the way things are but would be willing to experiment.
- *What are some of your favorite traditions?*
- List some possible traditions to incorporate into your day, week, or year—around a holiday, perhaps, or at breakfast every Saturday morning.
- Introduce a fun service activity your family could do together— you're not limited to serving in a soup kitchen, either.
  - If you love animals, find an animal therapy program that needs volunteers.
  - Check with your church to see if you can clean on Saturday nights before church.
  - A ministry that accepts donations might need people to sort, clean, and organize.
  - Check with a local nursing home, and see if you can bring your daughter in to paint the ladies' nails.
  - Volunteer for a week at a camp, helping with repairs and painting.
  - Even families with small children can pick up trash at the local park.
  - Help a neighbor with a project that she can't easily tackle alone.

Live from the Slow Zone: *Various Traditions of Slow Zone Contributors*

When my kids were little and we were holding hands, I'd squeeze their hand three times, and this meant, "I love you." They would grin back at me and squeeze my hand four times for "I love you, too." We still use this nonverbal communication even though the kids are older.

—Judy Vriesema

There is something intensely warm and nostalgic about tramping around the Christmas tree farm and bantering about the "strengths and weaknesses" of each evergreen—and then, somehow, arriving at a consensus to select our tree. Stephen whips out the saw and goes to work. Then we all run back to the tent to enjoy hot cocoa and cookies while our tree is wrapped for transport home.

—Susan Clark

We always decorate the birthday person's chair the night before the special day and put all the presents at his or her place. In the morning, we enjoy a special breakfast together.

—Andrea Birch

Decorating Christmas cutout cookies has become a tradition we look forward to all year. We've done it since our kids were so small that you never wanted to eat their germ-smeared cookies! It was disgusting, but fun. The last few years have been especially enjoyable since the older ones have come home from college just for the annual event.

—Rachel Anne Ridge

Each week on "Bagel Day," my husband takes one of the kids to a local coffee shop for a bagel breakfast. This is the kids' special time to connect one-on-one with Dad. By starting this tradition when they were young, we hoped it would lay the groundwork for the teenage years—when the conversations shifted from childhood dreams to teenage realities and struggles. So far, it has! Our fifteen-year-old daughter is just as comfortable sharing with her dad as with me.

—Sharon Stohler

When we travel for more than three or four hours, our family listens to books on tape. We went from *Adventures in Odyssey,* to *Narnia* and *Charlotte's Web,* to *Where the Red Fern Grows* and *A Day No Pigs Would Die*—and eventually to *Prairie Home Companion* and even some motivational tapes! This has created a shared experience, and we can stop it at any time to discuss where it might be going.

—Judy Vriesema

Our tradition is a four-day camping weekend in August, just before the kids go back to school. We call it "The Last Hurrah." Each day we set aside time to pray over each child as they face the new school year. It's a wonderful time to grieve together that summer is over, reflect on the Lord's faithfulness in each of their lives, and wait with anticipation of what He has for each of them in the year to come. It's especially good for my own heart, as it is my least favorite time of the year ... because I must let go, especially of those who now head off to college.

—Beth Pfister

13 Living at the Speed of Love

"Mama, can you play Sorry with me?" my little boy asked one afternoon. His sisters were at school, and he needed some attention.

I was focused on work and under a deadline. I glanced at my watch and estimated the time it would take. Board games are a slow and inefficient undertaking. I didn't have time for a preschool-paced game of Sorry.

"Not right now," I answered.

Don't ask me what crucial, time-crunching deadline kept me from playing Sorry with my young son, because I can't even remember. At the time, however, it seemed so vitally important that I couldn't take a break.

And after I completed that vitally important assignment, something else took priority—maybe an urgent phone call or a series of emails; I can't remember. My young son waited awhile, lingering near the board that he had carefully set up, grouping the pawns by color in their starting circles. He asked, "Now can you play?"

"Not now," I responded. Something else required my full attention.

Eventually he gave up on me and shoved Sorry back into the game cupboard.

That's when I looked up—when the cupboard door clicked shut.

I watched him climb onto the couch to flip the pages of *Horton Hears a Who*. He didn't complain. He didn't whine and groan. He just gave up.

His resignation stirred me.

I *do* work from home, and he knows it. He generally understands that I have deadlines and obligations, but I don't want to put him off indefinitely. I want to live slow enough to listen, to pay attention, to notice, to play Sorry with my son.

I want to live slow enough to love.

I want the children, too, to live at a pace that allows for love. I don't want them to miss opportunities to serve, pray, and play simply because they grew up in a blur, with hurry dominating their formative years.

That busy afternoon, I put on the brakes. I set aside my papers and planner and apologized. I left my computer monitor, joined him on the couch, and read *Horton Hears a Who*. And then we opened the cupboard and pulled out Sorry.

I can't remember a single deadline I was stretching or what email I delayed sending. I can't remember who phoned during the game, when I chose to let voice mail pick up.

What I remember instead—and I remember it vividly—is feeling him lean against me as he turned the pages of the book. I remember how excited he was to unfold the game board and set up the colors again. He let me choose, and when I picked yellow, he asked me to choose again. When I chose blue, he said I could be red. He laughed as he sent my red piece back to home base, shouting in a pseudo-sinister voice, "Sooorrrryyyy!" He moaned when I pulled a card with a big number, or slid across some free spaces, or turned one of my pawns into the safety zone. He shrieked with delight when he won. He danced. He made up a song.

I radically altered my pace in order to meet his needs. I had to choose, because my hurried state challenged and tempted me. I had to tell myself to slow down ... to take a break ... to stop.

Only then could I see clearly what was needed.

Only when I stopped, when I no longer hurried, could I move at the speed of love.

Go play a game with your family. Trust me: You won't be sorry.

Slow Notes

- Discover your family members' love languages[1] and try to do something special this week that specifically fits each one:
  - Words of Affirmation
  - Quality Time
  - Receiving Gifts
  - Acts of Service
  - Physical Touch
- Family Game Night: Pull out Sorry, Monopoly, Wii, or Uno, and have some fun. Oh, and if you're competitive, be sure to model gracious winning.
- Read Aloud: Reading aloud is a communal countercultural act— one that slows us down and pulls us together on multiple levels. Not only are we physically close, but we come together in the

story. The characters weave into our lives and become part of our shared experiences, form some of our corporate memories, and enter our family vocabulary. Reading picture books with little kids offers such snuggly moments of love, but don't stop reading aloud to your family when your child masters phonics.

- Find a slow setting: Curl up in front of the fireplace, pile onto the bed, sprawl in the living room, flop onto an old quilt spread on the grass, lounge in a hammock, or perch on logs while sitting around a campfire.
- Read poetry aloud at breakfast, short stories at lunch, or novels after dinner.
- I'm a sucker for classics, starting with picture books like *Make Way for Ducklings* and *Caps for Sale* and moving on to the Little House and Narnia books, *Anne of Green Gables, Heidi,* and later, *Lord of the Rings.*
- Read across genres—biography, science fiction, plays, historical fiction, nonfiction, adventure, and classic. (See www. NotSoFastBook.com for book lists.)

Live from the Slow Zone: *Lynn House*

Our firstborn, Poor Thing, was rushed here and there. Forced to stay on a schedule. Told not to touch this or that. Made to be our perfect little offspring. But he didn't want to be perfect, Poor Thing. He wanted to throw stones on the slide to hear them clang. He wanted to taste the cat food to see if the cat's food was better than his. He wanted to crawl out of bed at 10 p.m. to see what Mom and Dad did at that time of night. But instead of letting him listen to the clangs, or see that the cat food really wasn't all it was cracked up to be, or cuddle with us at 10 p.m., we squelched Poor Thing's curiosity and sometimes even his spirit. My heart drops into my stomach as I think about our call to perfectionism, and truth be told, our own avoidance of embarrassment as we were sure we would be judged by his behavior.

Thank God for putting our hearts over our egos … because three boys later, we have a child who is allowed to move at his own pace … at least most of the time.

I call it "moving at the speed of Jaden." He likes to look at things and ponder them. He stops to notice, to laugh, to play.

Moving at his speed is a gift. It opens my eyes to the things we adults often overlook. It's slowing down. It's our own personal slow "movement": Letting him jump off the giant rock at preschool … listening to his favorite part of *Star Wars* over and over and over and over (and that's not too many overs) … watching, actually watching, as he acts it out … staying after football practice so he can chase friends around the field … staying up past bedtime with him to finish the LEGO crane Papa just bought … snuggling on the couch for yet another chapter of an enticing book.

Thankfully, Poor Thing is only ten and perhaps we can undo some of the neuroses we may have created in him. Oh, how much better it is for the health and heart of all of us when we move at the speed of Jaden. It's so much better than the *Don't touch / Don't eat that / Hurry up / Find your shoes / Get in the car / We have to leave for football / What do you want from the McDrive-thru? / Have you finished your homework? / Let the dog out / Let the dog in / Put the dog in the crate / Get upstairs and brush your teeth / Get to bed NOW / I'm going to collapse on the floor now* kind of lives that we so often lead.

Instead, may most days move at the speed of a child filled with wonder![2]

14 High Cost of High Tech

Television. Computers. Handheld games. Video games. All those screens, screens, *screens!*

Television

Suppose someone showed up at our door offering to sell us a hypnotic device guaranteed to "pollute our children's morals, stunt their intellectual development, rob them of their imagination and likely lead them toward both obesity and poor grades. We'd likely run them off. Instead, we not only welcome them into our home, we make sure they set up their wares in every room in the house."[1]

It's the one-eyed babysitter. The boob tube. The plug-in drug. Flickering images from the TV screen serve as a tractor beam, latching onto our kids' attention and sucking them into worlds far from their family rooms.

And yet, in a way, the inert pose of a TV-watching kid could seem like just the thing to promote slowness ... all that sitting and staring sounds like the epitome of the slow life, doesn't it? The house is quiet. Nobody's arguing. All is still. What's not to love?

But, wait! Inert bodies and brains are *not* what the slow life is aiming for.

As we seek the right pace for our families, we're doing so in order to raise bright, focused, healthy, spiritual, hardworking, faithful kids who love the Lord and the people He's placed in their lives.

Television fights against all that. It shuts down interaction with flesh-and-blood family members and discourages active playtime with neighbors and friends. Even when playmates aren't available, I prefer getting the kids outside with each other, breathing in some fresh air, riding bikes, weeding the garden, or crunching leaves scattered across the yard.

But when the kids were little, I had desperate moments. I was weary; I needed a break.

So I flipped on the TV and tuned into PBS. In my ideal world, my little preschoolers would have been painting with finger paints and poring over picture books, but I was weak. Sometimes I let show after show run its course while I recuperated.

At some point along the way, however, I no longer needed that time … but the kids still expected their morning shows. One daughter in particular started to prefer television and videos to almost every other activity. That disturbed me. And I couldn't stand that dull, lifeless pose—three kids lined up on the couch staring at a screen, mesmerized by Elmo.

Worse yet, while kids may seem dull and lifeless in front of the television, research suggests that the constant, fast-paced flow of images stimulates heart rates and hijacks thought patterns. Lifeless on the outside masks the high-speed effects inside. Researchers aren't in accord on precisely how TV exposure affects development in young people, but some argue an actual rewiring might be occurring in young brains spending hours glued to the ever-changing pictures on the screen. Quick scene shifts on videos become "normal" to a baby when they aren't at all normal in real life, and various studies have been exploring links between early TV-watching habits and the development of such problems as obesity, aggression, asthma, autism, and ADHD.

Though the results don't agree completely, nearly everybody agrees that TV time needs to be limited and its content can be dangerous. Sexuality and violence are common in the content of both shows and commercials. Those messages and images encourage kids to consider topics unsuitable for their age—another instance of the world pushing kids to grow up too fast.

We could just turn off our TV sets. Or give them away. That's what some people have done, cutting off the influx of conflicting values.

As Philippe and I attempt to communicate our faith in Jesus Christ and commitment to love and purity, for example, a lot of messages and images contradict what we're passing along (in a much more attractive package)—children's programming isn't so bad, but even shows aimed at tween-aged kids include plenty of subtle messages woven into the dialogue, body language, clothing, and humor. If our kids catch a few minutes of a show intended for adults, even relatively tame programs include content that's relationally and sexually questionable.

Another downside to watching television is the discontent it encourages. It's not just the commercials, which can be skipped with TiVo; now story lines and characters themselves often communicate the desire for a steady flow of more, better, and *now.*

In general, an alarming amount of TV content tends to push kids to grow up faster, rushing them through childhood in pursuit of more sophisticated wares and experiences while celebrating both outrageous and subtle sins.

Philippe and I knew that radically changing our kids' viewing habits was best, but how to go about it? We gathered opinions from respected friends who made radical choices like not even owning a TV, and took note of the American Academy of Pediatrics' recommendation: absolutely no TV (later they said "screen time") for kids under the age of two and no more than two hours a day for kids over the age of two.

Even more alarming research confirms our decision to seriously limit exposure:

- Number of minutes per week that the average child watches television: 1,680.[2]
- Children are graduating from high school having logged twice as many hours in front of a TV as in a classroom.[3]
- Children are spending 90 percent of their TV time watching programs that were designed for adults.[4]
- The average child will watch 8,000 murders on TV before finishing elementary school.[5]
- By age eighteen, the average American has seen 200,000 acts of violence on TV, including 40,000 murders.[6]
- Percentage of Americans that regularly watch television while eating dinner: 66 percent.[7]
- Percentage of day care centers that use TV during a typical day: 70 percent.[8]
- Ninety-one percent of foods advertised to children are high in fat, sugar, and/or salt, which contribute to obesity and dental problems.[9]

- Children who consistently spend more than four hours per day watching TV are more likely to be overweight.[10]
- Kids who view violent events, such as a kidnapping or murder, are also more likely to believe that the world is scary and that something bad will happen to them.[11]
- TV consistently reinforces gender-role and racial stereotypes.[12]

We definitely wanted to slow down our kids' exposure to this technology. So we weaned the kids—and ourselves—from television.

One step was to move the TV sets away from the main floor: out of sight, out of mind. And it worked pretty well. The habit our little kids had formed was to roll out of bed, head straight for the family room, flip on the TV, and stare. Relocating the TV to a less accessible spot helped them stop thinking about it first thing—as an alternative, we made lots of toys like LEGOs, Lincoln Logs, and Playmobil readily available.

It was hard at first. They weren't thrilled with the new time restrictions or being limited to occasional nature shows and one movie—okay, sometimes two—a week. But they adjusted to the changes over time, and with maturity grew to appreciate our decisions. These days, even our two teenagers watch very little TV—one or two shows per week at the most.

Then and now, when we do watch TV, we try to watch it together and talk about the shows and ads (muting the worst offenders), evaluating out loud the values they promote, often dissecting them later. I suppose we steal a lot of the fun, but at least the kids are learning to slow down and analyze.

After TV detox, our kids grew as captivated by low-tech entertainment as they had been by *Sesame Street*. They read for hours and appreciated long stretches of quiet. They might get loud playing games, and their activities were much messier than TV watching, but at least they were engaged and active. I hated stepping on marbles, dice, and puzzle pieces, but I tolerated the creative chaos in the name of intellectual stimulation and healthy development.

Their minds were lively, and their eyes were fresh and focused.

That's a beautiful thing to a mom embracing the slow life.

Even now that they're older, as we continue limits on viewing, they still enjoy reading, writing stories, exploring, taking long walks, wading knee-deep in streams, feeding ducks, and rolling down hills. Just the other day, on a chilly late-winter afternoon when flipping on a show would have been a far simpler (and warmer) activity, I instead proposed a walk and heard a resounding "Yay!" One daughter would have preferred to curl up in front of the one-eyed babysitter, but she came with us. I ended up walking while they rode bikes. At the neighborhood playground, they created a game that was something like "Marco Polo," and then sat and swapped silly jokes. As they rode their bikes home, their cheeks were rosy. They were all smiling.

So was I.

Video Games

What a relief! We seemed to have successfully navigated the perils of television. All was well.

Until … games.

Our bright-eyed, perky, interactive children flourished in our low-tech home. When visiting high-tech friends, however, they plopped down on the floor, took hold of the video game controls, and entered an altered state. I found it disconcerting to watch my usually lively kids sit riveted to screens, engrossed in a virtual universe. Disengaged from reality—at least, reality as *I* think of it—they became fully engaged in a fast-paced game requiring swift response. The action of the games consumed them, even driving the speed of their heart rates as stress built during the play produces an adrenaline rush.

Fun is fine, but we didn't like the thought of constant exposure to this technology. Electronic games appeared to stunt creativity and waste natural learning opportunities, confining brain boosting to limited problem solving in a computer engineer's restricted framework. As a result, the gamer isn't free to make the kind of intentional choices life requires—there's only a hectic reaction to what's thrown in one's virtual path.

Everyday life seems sluggish and tedious by comparison. Gaming invigorates, requiring immediate response and reaction rather than true problem solving, leadership, group interaction, cooperation, restraint, and self-control. Gaming requires close attention, but not to endearing matters. Excessive game time allows machines to determine the speed at which a child's mind will operate, instead of kids naturally discovering the right speed for themselves. Kids accustomed to gaming speed will habitually reach for technology to maintain that brisk mental pace.

We wanted our kids to have the best chance of developing the habits of self-direction, self-reflection, and close attention, capable of thoughtful analysis and understanding as well as compassion for others.

Gaming seems to fly in the face of all that.

For years we resisted. Friends bemoaned game-driven tensions such as disagreements and arguments as well as time lost that could have been spent building snowmen, creating puppet shows, or playing catch. Their trials and tribulations served as cautionary tales; instead of binding families together, gaming seemed to cause division. We wanted to avoid that trouble and concluded that electronic games were too isolating and addictive to allow.

We were also concerned with the spiritual impact—or lack thereof. Minds obsessed with virtual reality of video games find a task as spiritually nourishing as memorizing and meditating on God's Word quite dull in comparison. They demand a kind of focus, but not on thoughts of one's choosing; they force fast-action, exciting thoughts instead of promoting God-centered thinking.

So, for years our poor, deprived children had no Xbox, Nintendo DS, or Game Boy. With all that game-free time on our hands, we hiked at the park and skipped rocks in the pond.

Then people would argue the *merits* of gaming:

- *"These gadgets really help kids develop quick problem-solving skills and outstanding hand-eye coordination."* They'd have to do better than that—we were successfully tapping into fun and low-tech ways to develop great hand-eye coordination.
- *"Games were key to motivating our youngest to read."* This family's child desperately wanted to read messages that popped up on the screen at critical junctures in a favorite game. Suddenly phonics practice had a direct application, and he was reading—and winning the game—within weeks. But we were pretty sure we could motivate our youngest to read without a gadget.

- *"We just returned from the most peaceful road trip ever—thanks to Nintendo DS, we logged mile after mile in blissful silence."* Oooo … now you've got my attention. Long stretches of quiet? A chance for Philippe and me to talk for miles uninterrupted? That almost sold us, but we wanted to stick to our resolution. On the next road trip, my kids, those lucky ducks, would fill out Mad Libs and listen to books on tape.

Then the kids started to beg for them. "Our friends all have Game Boys."

"I'm not paying one cent for a Game Boy," I said.

"We'll save up and buy one with our own money!" they negotiated. They asked for permission to work and save and cover the cost.

Our resolve weakened. When we spotted the opportunity to create a life lesson in economy, scrimping, saving, and budgeting (while dreaming of a peaceful road trip), we talked ourselves into it.

In other words, we caved.

We would allow games … under certain conditions:

1. Just as they offered, the kids had to raise the money entirely by themselves (hopefully before our next road trip).

2. As in all things, we retained the right to deny them the use of their gadget indefinitely. If, for example, they began to neglect their duties, fail to relate to each other or us, or in any way show obsessive tendencies, the games would be confiscated until further notice.

3. No violent games—or any with sexualized images (though
    we didn't state that out loud).

They agreed to these restrictions and saved, saved, saved. Then,
one day, the first child had enough to go shopping. As we drove to
the store, I reviewed the rules. She humbly accepted our limits while
counting her cash and preparing for the transaction of a lifetime.

She bought hers—a shiny blue Game Boy—and one by one the
others followed suit. Within a few months, they each had a new
Nintendo Game Boy and a few simple games—Mario, Narnia, and
Nintendogs.

All was fine. At first.

Because they'd worked so hard to earn enough for their treasured
games, they proudly explained how they acquired them when asked.
They "trained" each other's electronic dogs, asked for advice on how
to defeat the White Witch in the Narnia game, and raced each other
in Mario. They discussed strategies and helped each other through
particularly difficult levels. Most importantly, whenever I told them
to shut down, they immediately snapped shut the lid—no questions
asked, no lingering, no requests to play "just one more minute."
Good. We seemed to be managing these systems fairly well.

Gradually, however, the games became the first thing they'd reach
for. They upgraded to the Nintendo DS and DS Lite. They stopped
asking permission and began to assume it was okay to play whenever
they liked. Some of the kids grew obsessed with the games. They would
zone out. They stopped inventing real-life adventures and talking with
each other as much. We discovered that some of them would sneak
their games under their pillows to play at night. One of them even had

her system just out of sight with the sound turned off at the dinner table when we were visiting family. I was mortified.

Then we unearthed statistics and studies that made us regret we'd ever agreed to open such a Pandora's Box in our home:

- The American Academy of Pediatrics (AAP) recommends that children over age two years spend no more than two hours per day with screen media, including TV, because excessive viewing has been linked to a plethora of physical, academic, and behavioral problems.[13]

- A study conducted by the National Institute on Media and the Family concludes that watching lots of violence on television and playing violent video games makes kids physically aggressive, distrustful, and meaner (it correlates with "relational aggression," behavior that includes name-calling, making threats, and spreading rumors).[14]

- A Stanford University study found that when third- and fourth-graders' television and video game consumption was reduced to under seven hours per week for twenty weeks, their verbal aggression decreased by 50 percent and their physical aggression decreased by 40 percent.[15]

- More than three-fourths of games rated "E" for "Everyone" contain violent content. In half of these games, violence was significant to the plot.[16]

- Researchers recommend strict limits on screen time. A few experts warn that some people are genetically inclined to become addicted to the stimuli of video games.[17]

- Though the American Medical Association doesn't classify it as a formal disorder, more than 20 percent of kids in the United States are considered addicted to computer and video games, which

produce physiological reactions in the brain similar to those associated with substance abuse.[18]

- Research shows that the chemicals triggered by about thirty minutes of game play rival an amphetamine high.[19]
- Eventually, a process called "habituation" takes over—rewiring the
brain and creating a physiological dependence similar to cocaine
addiction. (The first detox center for video game addicts recently
opened in the Netherlands.)[20]
- The earlier a child begins playing electronic games, the sooner he
or she is exposed to the patterns that lead to addiction. [21]
- Those who are introduced to the dopamine-inducing high of prolonged
video game play often become bored with any other recreation.[22]

Were they addicted? It sounded extreme, but the kids were certainly exhibiting traits that researchers and experts warn about, so we
reeled them in, weaning them from screens once more.

With the exception of a recent road trip, they've not reached for them
first thing any longer. They still love to play—when permitted. They
compare notes with their cousins and friends. They've even been invited
to DS parties, where the kids all bring their handheld games and play
together. I reluctantly agreed to let one of my daughters, a fifth-grader at
the time, attend one of those with some good friends from school.

When I picked her up, I asked about the games.

"Oh, we hardly played them at all," she reported.

"Really?" I replied. "I thought it was a DS party?"

"It was, but we had too much fun playing in the woods behind
her house."

Ah ... music to my ears.

Computers and Internet

More screens. Sigh. This time we invited them into our home in the form of laptops.

For Internet safety and accountability, experts recommend that families have only one centralized computer in a public spot—a kitchen nook, perhaps, or on a desk in the family room—for easy parental monitoring.

This is exactly what we did for years. I had my own computer for work, but everyone else shared a big, old, Mesozoic-era PC that sat in the family room. It either locked up or ran excruciatingly slowly (yes, there *is* such a thing as too slow).

But we recognized that technology can be a powerful tool; so, one year, we decided to use a computer-based homeschool program. Ideally, each of the girls needed her own computer, so we invested in laptops for portability. They also needed Internet access—a possible danger, we knew. To keep in touch with European grandparents and cousins, we even allowed them to create email accounts.

But it all came with limits:

- We'd have access to their laptops at any time to read and review every site they visit and every email that they send or receive.
- Online games only at preapproved sites, none of which include online chats or discussions where personal information could be inadvertently revealed.
- No laptops in bedrooms.

This technology represents a rapidly evolving world that they must learn to navigate carefully, for fear of unseen dangers and temptations. For additional insight, I talked with a friend named Beth Pfister to hear how she handled it. Her two younger kids are in high school, and her two older kids are in college. She said that one way she's guarded her children's sexuality and slowed down their exposure is by limiting computer use. "Internet stuff is really, really scary," she said, "so we've been extremely countercultural. For example, my kids have never had a Facebook or MySpace page. In fact, Jacob still doesn't have one, and he's in college and will be twenty-one this spring."

Until they're out of the house, all of her kids' emails pass through Beth's inbox. "We try to respect their privacy, but I reserve the right to read everything in their inbox and sent box. The idea is that there shouldn't be anything that comes or goes in an email that they should be embarrassed or ashamed of."

Male-female email communication wasn't allowed until the later years of high school. If a young man wanted to talk to one of her girls, he had to phone. "That's because both online and in email, a false intimacy occurs far too often," Beth explained. "Sexual conversations and innuendo are happening over the Internet and in email at younger and younger ages, because even though it's not anonymous, it's not face-to-face."

One of her daughters broke the rule when she was in middle school. The girl got into a discussion online with a young man she knew. He detailed in sexually explicit language precisely what he wanted to do with his girlfriend. "She came to us in hysterics," Beth said, "and we prayed with her. But she broke the rule, and it did not go well. She learned the hard way why we set it in the first place—to protect her."

Beth's limits may seem extreme in this fast-paced, high-tech day and age, but as she said, if we want to slow down our kids' exposure to sexual images, content, interaction, and temptation, we're going to have to put the brakes on this, as well, and choose to counter the culture.

Beth and her husband, Jeff, host a high school gathering in their home on Friday nights. They teach a Bible lesson, lead a discussion, and then serve snacks for the kids as they relax playing darts and foosball. This heavily chaperoned, openly Christian event has been a draw for their kids' friends, providing a safe place to deepen friendships and explore Christianity. But it has also given Beth the privilege of hearing the struggles and issues that kids are facing straight from the source, solidifying her decision to place extreme limits on technology use in their home.

Her choices impressed me. As we look back at our errors and consider what's ahead, we've decided it's better to err on the conservative side and ease up later than to offer lots of freedom and have to rein our kids back in. With computer usage, we want to take the advice of people like the Pfisters. Their kids have no regrets or resentment that they were restricted. They're grateful.

Taming Technology

Technology is here to stay. Plus, it can be a powerful tool. I'm typing on a laptop at this very moment and love it. I use it for research and writing, email and blogging.

But I need to be very careful not to let it consume so much of my time that it steals too much from off-line, real-world relationships. Modeling restraint and restrictions is hard. Because I work from home, my usage is on display. Still, I want to demonstrate that I can walk away from it, so I'm watching myself. I want the kids to know that there's more to my life than facing a glowing screen all day, day after day.

The same kids who grew addicted to video games may struggle with computer addiction. We must tame technology in our household. We'll use it, but it's easier to place limits on all of us now and loosen up later than to loosen up now … and regret it for the rest of our lives.

With that in mind, I think I'll stop typing now, fix some dinner, and have a lively conversation with my family around the table. Tacos, anyone?

Slow Notes

- Ask your kids to list several activities they enjoy—riding bikes, a walk in the park, card games, reading—and then compare them against their favorite screen activity.
  - *What do you prefer: Riding bikes or playing a video game?*
  - *What's more fun: Monopoly or gaming?*
  - Their answers may surprise you. Electronics may trump all other activities, or you (and they) may realize that there are dozens of fun things they like better.
- Set media limits. Use a timer. Proclaim a "no-tech" day. Provide plenty of low-tech options.
- Consider the Pfisters' ideas:
  - Run all emails through one account.
  - No Facebook or MySpace.
  - Parental controls and Internet filters.

- Interested young men or women must use the phone, not email, to interact with your daughter or son.
- One computer for all to share in a common room—and no computers in bedrooms.
- Declare a letter-writing day. Pull out stationery, pens, and stamps. Communicate the old-fashioned way as a positive protest against technology. Write to each other, friends, grandparents, pen pals, or soldiers.

Live from the Slow Zone: *Trish Southard*

We don't have all the electronic stuff that other families have. What we do have is flour. I bought twenty-five pounds of flour for my daughter, Sabrina, because she loves to bake, and I've found that it makes her attractive to her friends. The neighborhood girls come over and instead of doing "Dance, Dance Revolution," they bake. They love our totally low-tech fun. They get free rein over my kitchen to be creative and make chocolate chip cookies, a cake, or any kind of muffin. And what's crazy is that we're *novel* for offering this. Not long ago I hosted a tea, and Sabrina volunteered to make three batches of scones all by herself. You know, if she had the gadgety stuff that all the other kids have, I don't think she would know how to do that.

15 Speeding Past Creation

The kids and I walked to a nearby pond that was frozen over. Near the edges, the ice was thinner, and the kids discovered that they could chip at the edges with a stick and break off ice chunks. The kids worked diligently, piling the chunks behind them for later use. Then two of the kids set off toward the line of trees to spear leaves, pretending they were hunting for food in the deep, wintry wilderness. "It's fresh kill," they said. Handy.

Before long, the two warriors abandoned their hunting and returned to the edge of the pond, where their two tamer siblings contemplated the possibilities. Soon, ice chunks became the main draw, and they all returned to chipping and piling up a stash.

I listened to the Shagbark hickory branches creak and sway while the kids hurled chunk after chunk of ice, watching them pop and skid across the hard, frozen surface of the pond. Some of the chunks would shatter. Some slid into a melted section near a drain. Some swooshed across to the other side of the pond. After awhile, the kids used their sticks to shove some chunks forward, like a game of shuffleboard or curling, watching their polygon pucks slide toward the middle of the pond.

We took our time; our afternoon was open. Had we packed our entire week and moved at a fast clip, it would have been hard to linger.

In our early days of parenting, while considering home education, I read a book by Charlotte Mason, a British educator from the
late 1800s. I was struck by her recommendation that kids be outside for several hours every day—four to six hours! On a chilly day,
she said, just pull on a heavy jacket and go outside anyway. Mason
saw taking walks, creating nature notebooks, dining al fresco, and
participating in outdoor exercise as important elements of a child's
overall education, critical to developing his body, mind, and soul. I
loved that! I took inspiration from her and attempted to encourage
my children's interest in and respect for God's creation.

In fact, when I looked back on my own life, I realized that many
intimate moments with God occurred in His natural world instead
of in a man-made setting. I felt sure that my kids needed to be out
interacting with nature so that the beauty of God's creation wove
into their childhood memories and learning. Besides, I loved that
they'd get all that fresh air and exercise. I wanted them to feel comfortable observing insects, plants, trees, animals, and weather. As we
all learned to appreciate God's handiwork, we grew more attentive,
observant, curious, and interested in taking care of it.

Compared to the majority of society, however, I felt like I was
often alone in this commitment. What seemed perfectly normal and
healthy to us turned out to be countercultural. The high-speed lifestyle
of most families doesn't mesh well with the slower pace of nature.

If a family actually manages to make time to get outdoors,
patience is required to make the most of it. When we're out walking,
for example, or watching birds at the feeder, or wading in a stream,
we must move slowly enough to wait and watch. Kids accustomed
to constant motion and continual entertainment struggle to find the

patience to plant a seed and wait for it to sprout, or to focus long enough to quietly study a praying mantis creeping along a stalk of fountain grass. Some adults find it dull, as well, and question it: *What's the point? There's nothing to show for it!* We're used to instant results and nonstop change. Appreciating nature requires a slower mind-set than our culture promotes.

Also, it seems that a lot of families prefer to be removed from the grit of sand and soil. They don't like to risk getting mucky or wet, passing on an "ick" attitude to their children. They worry that if they encourage outdoor time, their kids will end up with their new sweatshirts stained and caked with mud, and there's too much laundry as it is from organized sports. *I don't have time for that!* What if they bring home a dead butterfly or a bag of rocks and want to display them on the kitchen counter? What if they want a pet rat? Or an ant farm? *Yuk,* those parents think. *No, thanks!*

They may even find that electronics are a tidy alternative— statistics suggest that we're all choosing some form of electronics as our leisure activity of choice. These families may find nature dull and boring by comparison. Set them down in a state park, and they don't know what to *do,* preferring the vicarious action of their avatars. Besides, when kids are playing a Wii game or "Dance, Dance Revolution," they stay clean, get a bit of exercise, there's no mess, no one complains about being bored, and everybody knows exactly where they are—safe and sound, indoors. Nobody's going to get scratched up or fall into a ravine if they're sitting on the couch playing Xbox.

An issue for working parents is that they often arrive home late— certain times of the year, after dark—and until they get home, the kids stay indoors. The sitter may not be comfortable bundling everybody up to go for a walk; it is, after all, easier to keep track of everybody when they're in the family room. Then, during the flurry of homework and bath time, nobody even thinks to sit on the front stoop and catch the last streaks of rose and orange fading from the setting sun; nobody stops to watch the first evening stars appear.

Experts, counselors, sociologists, and educators are starting to notice how detached we are from nature; they're wondering if this next generation of kids will grow up able to rock out with "Guitar Hero" but won't be able to skip a rock. That the kids will recognize Kate Moss, but not the moss that grows on trees, stones, and forest floors.

Kids are growing up "denatured," they say. Author Richard Louv has warned that kids are growing up with "Nature Deficit Disorder."[1] Others are seeing a kind of "eco-phobia" or "biophobia" in kids as they disassociate with nature and avoid it—even fear it. "Biophobia ranges from discomfort in 'natural places' to active scorn for whatever is not manmade, managed, or air conditioned." We also see biophobia in the tendency to regard nature as nothing more than a disposable resource.[2]

We already cited possible contributors to "biophobia"—fast-paced lives coupled with the tendency of kids (and adults) to spend more of their leisure time inside with electronics. Another reason may be our incessant talk of climate change, endangered species, and earth's potential doom—it can be overwhelming and hopeless to school-age kids who grow up with the message that it's too late, that the damage has been done, that it's pretty much over. In Christian circles, teaching about the end times can also leave alert kids wondering why they would want to stop the car to rescue a turtle in the road or take time to plant a tree that will take years to grow—if it's just a matter of time before this world ends, why bother?

But the more removed we get from God's creation, the more we risk losing perspective.

Psalm 8 begins, "O LORD, our Lord, how majestic is your name in all the earth! You have set your glory above the heavens.... When I consider your heavens, the work of your fingers, the moon and the stars, which you have set in place, what is man that you are mindful of him, the son of man that you care for him?" (Ps. 8:1, 3–4). As David considered creation's grandeur and beauty, his response was to praise the Creator. The psalm begins and ends the same way—with a right perspective of who we are in relation to who God is: "O LORD, our Lord, how majestic is your name in all the earth!" (Ps. 8:1, 9).

Isaiah, too, referred to the night sky—to part of creation—when he wrote, "'To whom will you compare me? Or who is my equal?' says the Holy One. Lift your eyes and look to the heavens: Who created all these? He who brings out the starry host one by one, and calls them each by name. Because of his great power and mighty strength, not one of them is missing" (Isa. 40:25–26). When we appreciate creation, we can celebrate the Creator.

Jesus was outdoors a lot. He taught in a boat and on a mountain, prayed in a garden, retreated from the crowds to be alone in His creation, and regularly pointed to everyday, living, God-made things—fig trees, mustard seeds, sparrows, yeast, sheep, goats—to illustrate His teaching and direct our thoughts. "Consider the lilies of the field," He said, "how they grow: they neither toil nor spin; and yet I say to you that even Solomon in all his glory was not arrayed like one of these" (Matt. 6:28–29 NKJV). Jesus' messages and parables are timeless not only in principle, but also literally: *Look at what God has made. Look and learn.* Consider the beauty of this grass that is cut down and thrown into the fire … consider, and be grateful, for God cares for us.

When we speed past creation, past the natural things that only God can make, we miss out on a huge part of who God is and how He views, sustains, and cares for us. "Since the creation of the world, God's invisible qualities—his eternal power and divine nature—have been clearly seen, being understood from what has been made, so that men are without excuse" (Rom. 1:20). The world He created points to Him; that is, He reveals Himself, in part, through the beauty, power, intricacy, order, and wildness that He Himself created. Psalm 19:1–4 suggests the same, that the "heavens declare the glory of God; the skies proclaim the work of his hands. Day after day they pour forth speech; night after night they display knowledge. There is no speech or language where their voice is not heard. Their voice goes out into all the earth, their words to the ends of the world." Creation is speaking of the one, true God, proclaiming His work, displaying knowledge of Him as our Creator.

Some of my friends are intimidated by nature. They don't know a tulip poplar tree from a sycamore. To encourage them, I often pass along a quote from Rachel Carson: "If a child is to keep alive his inborn sense of wonder … he needs the companionship of at least one adult who can share it, rediscovering with him the joy, excitement, and mystery of the world we live in."[3]

We don't have to be experts on flowers, chipmunks, or carpenter ants to rediscover with our child the joy, excitement, and mystery of the world we live in. All our kids need is our companionship as we sit alongside them and learn as we go. We can take pictures of unfamiliar flowers, fungus, bugs, or birds and show them to a park naturalist or compare them with photos in an identification book or online. If we adults demonstrate a tiny bit of interest and curiosity, we can build memories together with our children.

To encourage parents to actually get outside with their kids, Connecticut state officials launched a "No Child Left Inside" program in 2006, encouraging visits to parks among other things. The National Wildlife Federation promoted the "green hour," saying that kids need a casual hour outdoors every day in the same way that they might need a vitamin or a good night's sleep. Just as Charlotte Mason noted over a century before, experts are telling parents to get their kids outside.[4]

When I was a kid, I watched a good amount of TV, but I also caught butterflies, poked sticks into puddles, and lay in the barn loft on the farm where I grew up, so I may be more comfortable with the thought of coming inside with muddy shoes and flecks of hay stuck to my clothes. I scraped my knee and elbow as a kid and doctored it myself before heading out to continue playing. I collected buckeyes at the back of our property line, pulled apart honeysuckle flowers to taste the nectar, chewed sweet clover, and tried to breathe through a reed while swimming in a neighbor's pond.

That relaxed rural setting is also where the Lord introduced Himself to me. I came to understand His plan of salvation over time, often while kicking dirt clods in one of the fields. Being outside in a natural setting helped me really connect with the Lord and humbly acknowledge His power as Creator and Sustainer, while preparing me to eventually hear and accept my need for a Savior and Lord.

Those are my memories from an inimitable upbringing, yet I want to offer my children some aspects of that life. I want to actively create opportunities for them to find their own special, secret spots and imaginary worlds under a hedge or in a tree. I can't let them wander alone in our suburban setting, but we do what we can. The other day, we walked to our neighborhood park, where they rolled down a hill—and straight into some mud. I let them collect pinecones, acorns, walnuts, and piles of pebbles and rocks that we store on garage shelves. I don't turn every outing into a nature or spiritual lesson, but if something takes my breath away, I'll say so. We spent time at a nature center's bird observation area where the kids admired the chickadees and downy woodpeckers flitting from feeder to branch to the snow-covered ground. My youngest took my hand, led me to the window, and pointed. A red-tailed hawk balanced on a branch.

One winter day I took the kids for a walk to the neighborhood playground in unseasonably warm weather. They wore rubber boots and splashed in puddles all the way there and back. Later, as we kissed good night, they were all smiles. "That was so fun, Mama!" one of them exclaimed. "I loved feeling my boot get stuck in the sand at the volleyball pit. It made that big suction sound when I pulled it out."

Little children can woo us into the woods again, where we can appreciate our Lord's handiwork. If you slow down and spend time building memories outside, perhaps you will have a Mother's Day like most of mine.

Maybe, like me, you will receive gifts of love from the outstretched hand of your preschooler:

a fistful of daisies

wilted dandelions

or even dried up whirligig seed pods from a
maple tree.

Tuck the collection into a vase.

Position it front and center on the table.

Don't compare with other moms who got champagne brunches,
a bouquet of traditional carnations, or a dozen roses.

Water the daisies. Display the dandelions. Welcome the whirligigs. They came from the child, not Visa.

Then one day, two or three weeks later, take the child by the
hand, grab that vase of whirligigs, head into the backyard, and with
her permission, toss them high into the air.

Watch them spin.

Catch some.

As they wiggle down and tumble into your hair, laugh and be
amazed.

Life, love, joy, laughter, delight, wonder, and whirligigs.

Who knew that this could be your life?

Slow Notes

Think about a time when you appreciated something that only God
can make. Describe it in your Slow Notes, remembering how that
place or thing felt, smelled, looked. Thank God for creating it.

• Schedule an outing with a friend to a state or county park.

- Plant a container garden.
- Feed the pigeons.
- Rig up a bird feeder and watch sparrows, chickadees ... and squirrels.
- Plant a garden that provides an inviting refuge for wildlife. Add birdbaths and feeders.
- Provide a few gadgets that help kids think about the impact of rain and wind, like a homemade whirligig, thermometer, rain gauge, wind sock, or sundial.
- Invest in a child-size shovel or rake and show kids where they can use them.
- Let kids use the hose to water the plants.
- Make the most of other times your family is outside. While a child is at soccer practice, for example, walk around the fields with her siblings.
- Keep a nature journal, sketching flowers, trees, insects, and clouds.
- Lie on your back and watch clouds slide across the sky.
- Stay up late one warm night, lounge on blankets, and stare at the stars. Learn the constellations.
- Be inspired by nature-loving authors like Annie Dillard, James Herriot, and Gerald Durrell—grow in your appreciation of creation through their trained eyes and find yourself awed by the Creator of it all.
- Visit the zoo.
- Plan a vacation that includes a natural wonder you rarely see—geysers, hot springs, caves, mountains, waterfalls, canyons, icebergs, or oceans.

- Eat outside whenever possible. Pile on a sweater or coat in the fall. Throw a blanket on the ground and picnic.
- When weather permits, open the windows in your house and roll down the windows of your car.
- Read and meditate on Psalm 104.

16 Slowing Down Spending

Even during a recession, "shopaholics" embrace their obsession as a badge of honor—after all, the nation depends on them to rescue the economy with their wallets. Their mottos—"Shop 'til you drop" and "Whoever said money doesn't buy happiness didn't know where to shop"—are proudly displayed to the world on T-shirts, purses, and bumper stickers. These messages make us laugh as they attempt to justify habitual outings to the mall.

Compulsive buying is not viewed as anything startling or worth worrying about. It's not seen as a true addiction. Rather, "retail therapy," where shopping serves as an emotional comfort or consolation following some disappointment, is a widely accepted right of the female shopper. Consume in order to meet an emotional need—it offers a reassuring sense of pleasure and power to drive home with a trunk full of stuff after suffering a setback in some other area of life. When the outing turns social, all the better! Shopping with friends adds the pleasurable elements of connection, consultation, and conversation.

The shopping habit often needs financial backing of additional income, however, further increasing the pace of life for families. We accelerate, feeding the dissatisfaction that cries, "More, better, faster, and *now!*"

We think that it's fine—until our kids start asking for things. They beg. They fuss. They throw a fit. And we're frustrated and surprised, wondering why they can't accept no for an answer. Where did they learn dissatisfaction and this insatiable hankering for whatever catches their eye?

Without realizing it, we've contracted the virus of materialism in the land of "affluenza," and we're passing it along to our children. Delayed gratification—a slower approach to consumption—is nearly impossible in our credit-dependent culture. Kids don't learn to wait or save; instant gratification is central to most shopping outings. Spending is rushed—and spending *is* a rush.

Kids are growing up shoppers. *Impatient* shoppers, at that.

As babies and toddlers, they cruised through malls, strapped into their strollers, witnessing adults' desires for more, bigger, better, newer. They learned the effectiveness of fussing. If they pestered long enough, they got the desired response; the parent couldn't stand it and eventually gave in, buying the gum, stuffed animal, or Matchbox car to avoid a scene and calm the restless native. So the child learned that nagging and pestering really pay off—he got what he wanted, on the spot. As the child perfects these skills, marketers reinforce and encourage them more and more.

The "Nag Factor," or "Pester Power," is an openly discussed approach among marketers. At Heinz, a senior brands manager for their catsup division admitted to the *Wall Street Journal*, "All our advertising is targeted to kids. You want that nag factor so that seven-year-old Sarah is nagging Mom in the grocery store to buy Funky Purple. We're not sure Mom would reach out for it on her own."[1]

Similarly, a woman who directs strategy for a company called Initiative Media explained, "If we could develop a creative commercial—you know, a thirty-second commercial that encourages the child to whine ... that the child understands and is able to reiterate to the parents, then we're successful."[2]

If companies can get children to pester us to purchase, they've won. One source said that children influence an additional $670 billion worth of parental spending, making them a prime advertising target.

A national survey commissioned by the Center for a New American Dream expands on this idea:

- American children aged twelve to seventeen will ask their parents for products they have seen advertised an average of nine times until the parents finally give in.
- More than 10 percent of twelve- to thirteen-year-olds admitted to asking their parents more than fifty times for products they have seen advertised.
- More than half of the children surveyed (53 percent) said that buying certain products makes them feel better about themselves. The number is even higher among twelve- to thirteen-year-olds: 62 percent say that buying certain products makes them feel better about themselves.
- Nearly a third of those surveyed (32 percent) admitted to feeling pressure to buy certain products such as clothes and CDs because their friends have them. Over half of twelve- to thirteen-year-olds (54 percent) admitted to feeling such pressure.

• The nagging strategy is paying dividends for kids and marketers
  alike: 55 percent of kids surveyed said they are usually successful
  in getting their parents to give in.[3]

That's a lot of pestering!

But kids don't have to rely exclusively on their parents as walking ATMs. Our fast-paced world provides kids with impressive
financial resources once available only to adults. Even very young
children have spending money thanks to hefty allowances combined
with generous birthday gifts from aunts and grandparents. Often
they're entrusted with more than they can manage wisely on their
own. If the only advice they received was parental, perhaps they'd
have a chance. But they're targeted. Colorful and clever voices are
appealing to our children, advising them on the best use of their
available monies.

Yearly budgets for advertising and marketing aimed specifically
at children have exceeded $15 billion. This investment reflects the
buying power of children, now estimated at more than $30 billion
a year in direct purchases.[4] A leading expert on branding claims that
80 percent of all global brands now deploy a "tween strategy."[5] It
comes at them from all directions, too.

The average American child today is exposed to an estimated
forty thousand television commercials a year—over a hundred each
day, not counting product placement.[6] Soft drinks have invaded
schools. Corporations of all kinds send posters and provide educational resources that financially strapped schools can use to enhance
their curriculum—resources that happen to be stamped with the
companies' products, logos, slogans, and mascots. Channel One,

which broadcasts news summaries and educational segments each morning in eight thousand schools to over six million students, includes numerous ads targeted to its captive young audience.[7]

Everywhere they turn, kids are told to buy, to shop, to want more. They're urged to snatch up everything that catches their eye, everything they're told they need to be cool and accepted.

Not only are they buying lies about self-worth and meaning, but they also face other unwanted consequences. Relationships become strained when parents hold the line and refuse to buy. Conflicts erupt over disagreements about appropriate purchases. If a parent gives in, family finances may suffer.

Marketers try to convince us we don't have enough of something or don't have the right kind; they woo us to upgrade to the new-and-improved version. They love for stuff to become our obsession, our idol. They don't care if it pulls us away from the God who owns the earth and all it contains.

In our consumer culture, it's nearly impossible to be content.

But contentment counteracts consumerism.

Contentment can slow down spending.

"Keep your lives free from the love of money and be content with what you have," the author of Hebrews advises, "because God has said, 'Never will I leave you; never will I forsake you'" (Heb. 13:5).

Contentment and satisfaction come not from having stuff, but from having the Lord—we have all that we need in Him. Always. But it's so easy for "the deceitfulness of wealth and the desires for other things" (Mark 4:19) to slip in. The desires for other things are strong. We want the Lord, yes ... and maybe a few other things as well.

To promote contentment at a practical level, Philippe and I have attempted (with varying degrees of success) several things:

- Minimize media input, especially that which is riddled with commercials.
- Almost no television.
- Parent-approved music recordings in place of radio.
- Avoid items with characters emblazoned on them (Dora the Explorer toothpaste, Shrek yogurt). Those items are generally more expensive and less healthy—all the more reason to choose a store brand or something neutral. Mascots and cartoon stars grace the front of so many T-shirts and backpacks that it's hard to avoid. We try.
- Offer modest allowances—enough to learn to budget and save, but not so much that they can buy big-ticket items without some discussion and work.
- Unless it's true, we don't say, "We don't have money for that." I used to phrase it that way, and then realized it wasn't really true. We probably had enough money to buy certain items; we're simply not choosing to direct our resources to them at this time. Otherwise, kids get the idea that we simply need more income to get the things they want.
- Have them save for toys and gadgets. The thing they begged me for when we were rolling through Target may lose its magic when they have to save up for it. They begin to discern their most desired items.
- When we've bought a well-made, stylish outfit at the start of school, and they want the same thing with a name-brand stuck on it at

a ridiculously jacked-up price, we ask them to pay the difference (though we've given special items as gifts). The kids must decide: Is the logo (and pressure to wear it) worth that much more?

- We rarely shop. My DNA seems to be missing the shopping gene. I can't remember the last time I went to a mall with the kids.

- Shop secondhand. By shopping first for our needs (and a few of our wants) at Goodwill:

  - We aren't reinforcing advertising efforts or contributing unknowingly to sweat shops or unfair trade.

  - We're supporting recycling.

  - We encourage delayed gratification and contentment—if they don't find the thing they're looking for, we wait.

  - We aren't relying on sales to save money, which requires a shopper to frequent stores and malls, facing the temptation to buy treats and impulse purchases while browsing.

  - We enjoy occasional surprises—for my daughter's bedroom, we found a Pottery Barn bedspread (over $100 new) for $12.99.

- Suggest a giving strategy that equates with purchases. For example, two of our kids agreed to save double the amount needed for a Webkinz so that they could not only buy a new animal but also donate a mosquito net through Compassion International.

- Remind them (and ourselves) that God owns it all. The cattle on a thousand hills are His—as is every dollar in our pockets.

- Pray that the Lord will be their one desire. As my children walk more closely with the Lord, I pray that their hearts start to seek Him above all else—and *things* start to fall into perspective.

- Emphasize gratitude.

- We've tried to train our kids from a young age to respond with "thank you" to every gift and gesture of kindness. It's not exactly heartfelt when they say it out of habit, but at least it's said.
- Say "thank you" often *to* our kids when they help with something or give—so they hear gratitude expressed.

We're attempting to counter dissatisfaction by raising grateful, patient, content kids in a consumer culture. We're not sure it will work. Our kids may hit a certain age, take a part-time job, and go on ridiculous spending sprees with their earnings. And one of the kids just admitted she'd love to be a millionaire. They may grow up and indulge themselves in all the things we wouldn't buy for them when they were young. Time will tell.

We've made these choices, but our countercultural, countercon-sumerism life is about more than avoiding the mall and sticking with a budget. At the heart of it is the Lord. I want to set my mind and heart on things above, on Christ Himself, not on earthly things (Col. 3:1–3). I hope the kids do too.

If our children grow captivated by Christ, the stuff of this world will naturally lose its grip. They'll see how temporary it all is—how it's all going to end up at the curb for trash pickup. "The world and its desires pass away, but the man who does the will of God lives forever" (1 John 2:17). By living at a pace that allows time to know God and be consumed by Christ, we can let Him fill us with much more than we attempt to gain from the Stuff Mart.

In our fast-paced, forward-thinking, modern world, old hymns can seem quaint and trite. Some, however, I find to be simple yet powerful:

Turn your eyes upon Jesus,
Look full in His wonderful face,
And the things of earth will grow strangely dim,
In the light of His glory and grace.[8]

Instead of rushing to the mall in search of satisfaction, I will sit at the Savior's feet and look to Him to satisfy my deepest desires.

I hope that things I thought were so necessary will grow strangely dim.

One day I hope that we can all say, "That'll do. That's enough. My God has met all my needs according to His glorious riches in Christ Jesus."

He is enough. He is *more* than enough.

Slow Notes

Feel free to try the ideas our family has attempted. Also:

- Consider "compacting." A group of environmentally concerned friends in California signed a "compact" that they drafted, resolving not to buy anything new for a year (each family determined its exceptions, like underwear and toilet paper). They started an international trend. It's not a Christian movement, but the experience can change the way you view consumption. Milder variations? Buy nothing new for a month or nothing at all for a week.

- Count your blessings. Sit down as a family with your journal(s) and write out blessings. Keep track. Start thinking about what you've been given, not what you want to get. Be thankful.
- Give away. Not just to Goodwill, but also to friends and family. If a friend admires something in your home, consider wrapping it up and giving it to her. Experience freedom from the stuff you own.
- Enjoy the simple (and free) things in life. Express your pleasure over a bouquet of daisies, a warm shaft of sunshine cutting across the breakfast table, and a hug.
- Sing "Money Can't Buy Me Love."

Live from the Slow Zone: *Sara Janssen*

When I committed to The Compact in October of 2006, I had no idea how radically it would change my life. I simply set out on a mission to stop buying new stuff. But it went far beyond that basic goal: The experiment changed my entire view of our consumerism-obsessed culture, marketing, wants vs. needs, giving vs. selling, the poor … the list goes on and on. While I did not complete the entire year of Compacting by my "rules," I will be forever changed by this experience. Here are some effects of The Compact that are still with me today:

- I *love* buying used. It's almost physically painful for me to buy things new/full retail cost. I could spend hours and hours at Goodwill … especially if I have a list of things I've been looking for. The thrill of the hunt is so fun. Whenever we need something—whether it be items for the RV, clothing, kitchen gadgets—we always turn to eBay,

Craigslist, or Goodwill first before ever looking for it new. I would have to say that this *one thing* has been the biggest change for us.

- I've become appalled at the price of things and have started to realize the crazy profit companies make on our purchases because we are just too lazy to search out the alternative. My current pair of jeans (yes, I only have one pair) was ninety-nine cents at Goodwill. Matt found them for me in the men's section and said, "Here, honey, these will be cute on you." I *love* them! And now when I go in and browse the jeans, a tag for $3.99 seems ludicrous! How dare they think they can charge $3.99! This also happens when I've been to too many garage sales. I get used to the *low, low* prices, and it's hard to go back to eBay or consignment stores after that!

- I started to give a lot more stuff away. I think that when you come to the realization that it's the *stuff* that is bogging you down emotionally, mentally, and physically, you just want to get rid of it! So I got very good at filling boxes and going to Goodwill. Is there anything that feels better than handing over boxes of stuff that has been cluttering your home to the Goodwill attendant in the back of the store? I love it; it's a natural high!

- Handmade gifts are where it's at; if it's a handmade/recycled/found object art gift, even better! I think it was during my Compacting days that I discovered Etsy. Oh my goodness. How can you not love Etsy?[9]

- I am so much more sensitive to the marketing teams whose main goal is to make me feel like my current state of being is not good enough. They want me to want something. They scheme all day long by putting "want creators" on TV, Internet, billboards, junk mail … it's rampant.

- Because I am more sensitive to these things, I can hardly stand to set foot in a mall. The bright lights, the busyness, the insane amounts of money being exchanged. It's overload.

- I can now walk into a Target or any other store and actually only buy what I went in for. Prior to The Compact, I almost felt like a zombie as I walked out of Target, wondering what just happened in there! Last night, we went as a family to buy a few items that we've had on our list for weeks. And it felt so good to come out with just a few things on the receipt.

- Now that my daughter, Bella, is at the age where she can understand purchasing, money, wants, etc., it has become more time-consuming to go into stores because I need to discuss everything with her as we go. She amazes me with her self-control, though. When we walk by the dollar section in Target, she likes to stop and look but is not thrown into a frenzy if we decide not to get something there. We talk through it, and the experience becomes a teaching moment about consumerism, money, and priorities. We talk about whether or not we need it: Does she already have something similar? And if we were to get that item, would she be willing to give something else in her toy box away to make room for it? Young minds are hungry for teaching—and I try as hard as I can to teach her things that aren't in a normal school syllabus! Of course, it's pretty rare that we even go to Target, so I think this is the key to success. Keep children focused on the abundance they *do* have … not what they don't have. Gratitude breeds contentment.

And oh what joy will come if we can learn contentment! Pray for it … Christ wants to give it to you![10]

17 Slowing Down Sexuality

There are times when slowing down our families feels like a battle, as if powerful forces are working against us, yanking us back into the fast lane. Not only our families, but specifically our kids must deal with these ubiquitous forces, as practically the entire culture surrounds them with highly sexual messages, encouraging them to embrace mature themes at a shockingly young age. When it comes to sex and sexuality, our culture aggressively pushes kids to grow up fast.

In a *USA Today* article entitled "10 is the new 15 as kids grow up faster," Martha Irvine reported that tweens—ages eight to twelve—"listen to sexually charged pop music, play mature-rated video games and spend time gossiping on MySpace. And more girls are wearing makeup and clothing that some consider beyond their years.... Kids look and dress older. They struggle to process the images of sex, violence and adult humor, even when their parents try to shield them."[1]

Our kids are actively and strategically pursued by corporations and advertisers wanting to sell them something—clothes, music, movies, makeup, and games, many of which will utilize mature, sexually themed ideas at earlier ages than ever. Marketers have even coined some industry terms: "K.G.O.Y." (Kids Growing Older Younger) and "age compression" (pushing adult and teen products on young children). Acting on the reality that our highly sexualized culture pushes and entices kids to grow up fast, companies are creating products that are marketed accordingly.

Psychologist Susan Linn, author of *Consuming Kids: The Hostile Takeover of Childhood* and cofounder of Campaign for a Commercial-Free Childhood, explained, "Marketers say that kids are getting older at younger ages and market to 6-year-olds like they're 13, and 13-year-olds like they are 20…. As a result, children may be acquiring the material trappings of maturity, but their judgment and their cognitive and emotional development is [sic] not keeping pace."[2]

Even within this highly sexualized society, however, we have an opportunity to make significant decisions to slow things down. We can choose to limit exposure to media. We can talk openly with our kids, encouraging them to slow down and stay pure—to be *in* the world and love their friends and neighbors compassionately without being *of* the world and rushed into situations that would leave them unsafe and scarred. As author Mary DeMuth urges, we need "to engage as a family in people's lives in such a way that beckons them to Jesus Christ without sacrificing our family to the world system. We must model and teach this to our children. Engage in the culture, yet remain unstained."[3]

Let Your Requests Be Known to God

I wish that I could guarantee sexual purity for all four of my kids, but there's no formula for child rearing that guarantees a godly child. There's no one-size-fits-all approach or foolproof method for producing a self-controlled, pure, modest, Christ-centered teen or young adult.

Ultimately, children make their own decisions.

Sometimes without even trying, parents raise a child who sets strict personal standards and avoids premarital sex. Sometimes a Christian parent does everything "right," and her child chooses another path that leads to a highly sexual lifestyle. And there are stories of grace, where God brings beauty from ashes and shows His unconditional love and redemption by bringing good out of regret or even unwanted terrible, painful experiences.

The single most important way to slow down our culture's accelerated attitude toward sexuality is to pray. We pray desperately, depending on Christ every day—every moment. This is *the* key to this issue (actually, it's the key to *all* issues); the Lord is our only hope in this whole process. Our practical efforts, like delaying exposure to movies with mature themes, must be rooted in our own reliance on Christ as we call on Him to protect and direct us and our children. As we seek to find the right balance between engaging in the culture and remaining unstained, we pray, asking for His insight and wisdom, protection and strength. Our prayers for our children can echo Jesus' prayer for His disciples—and for us: "My prayer is not that you take them out of the world but that you protect them from the evil one" (John 17:15). As parents we seek to protect our children, but ultimately their path is in our heavenly Father's hands.

A Gardener Knows Her Seedlings

With the Lord's leading and empowered by His Spirit, we seek to determine the ideal pace, or speed, each child can handle. They can't be locked in a tower, like Rapunzel; in this fast-paced world that threatens to run over us, they can't be shielded from every sexual reference and image. However, we can make choices that protect and instruct, helping them understand within a Christ-centered, biblically grounded perspective. Again, as DeMuth reasoned, "We are to allow them to be children as long as possible, shielding them from adult themes, nurturing their innocence. But as in all journeys, the parent-child adventure changes over time. Sheltering progresses to instructing and eventually to releasing."[4]

My friend Judy Vriesema, an avid gardener, shared with me an analogy that has helped Philippe and me to guide our children through the twists and turns of daily life. We seek to know each child as we determine limits on what they can and cannot watch, listen to, or play. With Judy's permission, I'm expanding on her analogy a bit.

Children start out a lot like seedlings. A gardener puts her seedlings under a grow light and keeps them out of the elements when they're small and fragile. As plants begin to develop their root systems, we work them toward the goal of standing on their own, but every plant is different and has different needs; we learn what each can withstand. It's the same with kids—young children, especially fragile babies, need a protected environment to be safe and grow. As we work toward getting them established, we learn each one's unique personality and how much he or she can handle.

On a warm day, a gardener might take the sprouts and young plants outside—a process called "hardening off"—gradually preparing them to handle the big, wide world. As the temperature goes down, the hardier plants may stay out, but the most fragile ones have to come back inside. Rush the process, and some plants will suffer damage. But if the gardener takes her time and hardens them off little by little, each plant matures a little more and adjusts to the variable temperatures, natural sunlight, and even some rain showers.

As the seedlings get some height—and depth—the gardener prepares them for their future. When the plants are sturdy enough to handle it, she places them in the ground—still watching over and watering them, but less hands-on, with less hovering.

Some flowers and vegetables are strong and can handle being planted in the middle of the yard with the wind whipping against them and the dog digging nearby; those survivors are able to recover and be fine. But a more delicate flower needs to be sheltered from the wind and shielded from pets. For it to flourish, the gardener may plant it closer to the foundation of the home, let's say, or along the fence for added safety. Plants flourish when situated in the setting best suited for their strengths and weaknesses.

It's easy to see the comparisons. The process of raising strong children that are ready for the world is gradual, stretching over years and respecting each child's sensitivities. Rush the process, and some kids will suffer damage.

We have a tremendous amount of input over the influence our seedlings receive, and little by little we help them develop strong roots. A loving and prudent parent protects her child from what's inappropriate, observing his natural strengths and weaknesses, and how easily he is influenced. Is this child discerning? Can he stay strong against the pressures around him? Will this daughter go with the crowd or be a leader? As they develop and mature, we shift from watching over our kids to offering advice and setting limits, hovering less than we did when they were tiny.

One practical way to imagine how this analogy might play out is in the area of schooling. If it's feasible for the family to personalize each child's education, for example, one child may stand strong in a public school setting where sex talk among peers and even sexual acts are more common, while another may benefit from the more protected environment of a few years of home education or a smaller, Christian school.

An acquaintance recently described her eldest daughter, a public high school student. "I'm so proud of her," the mother said. "She stands up to some tough situations. Even some of her friends have caved in, but she's stayed strong. She's that kind of a girl—a strong person who's committed to the Lord. But my other daughter, I'm not so sure—we may consider another option. And our third is *so* sensitive; I'd homeschool him if I had the mind for it. Instead, we may look into a private school." She's sorting through her options to choose the best garden—in this case, the ideal school setting—for each of her children.

Parents have to make decisions about much more than schooling, however. Every party invitation and sleepover carries a question mark. The process of finding the appropriate amount of exposure is as tricky as finding the right speed. Again, it requires divine wisdom.

Help, Lord!

Clocking the Culture's Speed

Parents progress from sheltering their young children, to preparing them for inevitable exposure, walking them slowly through the confusion, eventually easing them toward independence. Some of us may be in the total sheltering stage of early parenting, while others are dealing with the effects of greater exposure. Regardless of what stage of parenting we find ourselves in, however, it's helpful to get a realistic view of what we're up against.

For decades, researchers have observed that children and adolescents, due to a lack of parental input or other information sources, turn to the mass media to learn about sexual behavior. Some go so far as to suggest that the media serve as the primary sex educators in American culture. This may very well be so. Consider this: Recent national surveys report that parents on average spend 3.5 minutes per week with their child in meaningful conversation, while youth ages eight to eighteen spend from six to nine hours a day with some form of mass media (including recorded music, television, movies, magazines, newspapers, and the Internet)—often alone in their rooms.[5]

When you do the math, it's easy to see who—or what—has the greatest input in kids' lives. And what are they learning?

From a young age, boys learn from all of these sources that they should be relentless in pursuit of women, while girls learn to view themselves as sex objects. Alone and curious, kids are composing their own scripts for romance and sexuality. With so much steady input, childhood is compressed; if we don't slam on the brakes, they'll be growing up way too fast.[6]

How can we protect their minds and slow down the fast-paced, highly sexualized input of images, ideas, and words? How can we counteract the degrading, misleading, dehumanizing messages thrown at them and instead help them view themselves—and others—as precious and valued human beings made in the image

of God, worthy of respect and protection? What can we do to help
them keep their way pure and live according to God's Word?

Monitor Myself

As I begin examining and measuring my kids' exposure to sexual
content and answering these questions, I have to start with myself. I
have to be honest: What am I watching and listening to? Do I model
self-control and restraint? How do I counteract the sexually charged
messages thrown at me? How do I view other people and what do
I say about them—do I speak respectfully of every person, even if
they're behaving contrary to my values?

Taking a hard look at my own habits and attitudes is a healthy
starting point for figuring out how to parent my kids in this area for
several reasons.

If I challenge them to watch, read, or view only material and
input that fits the criteria laid out in Philippians 4:8, could my media
diet stand up to the same scrutiny? Is it true, noble, pure, lovely,
admirable, excellent, or praiseworthy? If I question whether their
dress is glorifying to God, can I say the same about my own?

Most importantly: Do I model a vital relationship with Jesus
Christ, as one who is a devoted disciple, eager to honor God's Word
and do His will, and determined to weed out sin in my life? Everything
else must flow from that. If they, too, pursue a vital relationship with
the Lord, learning to listen to God and obey, they have more power
than my parenting attempts could ever supply.

At a practical level, I hope that as I seek to walk intimately with
the Lord, my daughters see in me the reality behind Proverbs 31:30:

"Charm is deceptive, and beauty is fleeting; but a woman who fears the LORD is to be praised." The state of my heart, soul, and mind is more important than the cut of my blouse or whether I've watched an R-rated movie. When I talk about purity and modesty, I want all our kids to see both Philippe and me living on a personal level what Paul wrote to the Ephesians, that in the church "there must not be even a hint of sexual immorality, or any kind of impurity" (5:3).

Do Not Keep Silent

Here's some encouraging news from researchers: Kids *do* listen to their parents. In fact, these secular researchers are finding that kids want to hear more from their parents. A recent survey found from kids themselves that it's very effective for parents to flat out say, "Don't do that." In the past, counselors encouraged reasoned conversations—and that's still an excellent approach to build relationships and connect with our children—but now they're seeing that parents who simply said, "Stop. We don't want you to do that," had the biggest effect in halting dangerous behavior.[7] By placing limits on our children's intake of sexually themed media and simultaneously maximizing our own input in our children's lives, we can create an environment that slows down their fast track to sexual sophistication before they're ready.

From early on, as we build a loving, respectful relationship with our children, we can offer a strong opinion and a firm voice in their ears. My friend Tish said that she took inspiration from a message given by an old-time preacher who took the phrase from Acts 18:9, "Do not keep silent," (NKJV) and applied it to parenting.

Tish explained, "When the boys are watching TV and something objectionable happens on one of the shows, I 'do not keep silent.' I say something right then, because the kids are watching, and they're wondering what I think. I want them to hear my opinion, so I'll sit there and say, 'I don't like the way she spoke to him. It seemed disrespectful. What do you think?' Or, 'I don't really think she's dressed appropriately, do you?' They hear my opinion immediately, and it gets them thinking about something they may or may not have noticed. It's led to some great conversations."

She and her husband have encouraged open dialogue with their sons, ages ten and thirteen. They've explained, "You need to always stay faithful to your wife—even though you haven't yet met her, you make decisions now to stay pure." Because they've demonstrated openness and clear leadership, Tish and her husband are able to talk with their sons about all kinds of topics openly and honestly as they've come up on an as-needed basis. The boys know where their parents stand and that they can ask questions without being shut down.

Our children are looking for leadership and direction and clarity in a confusing, sexually charged world. They want to hear from us, even if they act like they don't. And if we don't talk with them, there are plenty of other voices that will.

How Can a Young Man Keep His Way Pure?

A passage from Psalm 119 reads, "How can a young man keep his way pure? By living according to your word. I seek you with all my heart; do not let me stray from your commands. I have hidden your word in my heart that I might not sin against you" (9–11).

We can encourage our children from a very early age to counteract the effects of this highly sexual culture with the truth of God's Word. It's a purposeful way to slow down.

How does the verse advise young men and women to keep their way pure?

- By *living according to God's Word.* To do so, our kids can invest time in knowing God's Word. We can help with that, establishing the habit in our own lives to study the Bible and seeking to mine its treasure while urging our kids to do the same.
- We can *seek the Lord with our whole heart* and pray that our children will do the same. As they seek Him, they will know Him better, for He will be found—and He will seek them as well.
- We can ask the Lord to *keep us from straying from His commands.* In asking for His power, protection, and strength, we can see His work in our lives. Relying on Him in this way keeps our pride in check.
- Finally, we can *hide God's Word in our hearts* and teach our children to do the same. We signed our kids up for a club that emphasizes Bible memorization. For years, they've committed verses to memory. What starts as rote memory work for young kids can seep over time into their souls. I hope that they've learned to hide the living truths in their hearts!

We not only hide God's Word in our hearts—we also have God Himself in us. This verse speaks of a mind-boggling reality: "Do you not know that your body is a temple of the Holy Spirit, who is in you, whom you have received from God? You are not your own;

you were bought at a price. Therefore honor God with your body"
(1 Cor. 6:19–20).

The Holy Spirit is in us. We are not our own. We must seek to
honor God with these bodies that He bought at a price.

The Lord is at work in us and our kids. He who began a good
work in us will carry it on to completion until the day of Christ Jesus
(see Phil. 1:6). He has called us to be holy in all that we do, but our
righteousness doesn't come from restricting our TV-viewing habits
or turning off the hip-hop station. Our righteousness comes from
Jesus Christ Himself, through faith in Him.

Paul prayed the following for the Philippians—I'd like to pray
the same for us all:

> *And this is my prayer: that your love may abound more and more*
> *in knowledge and depth of insight, so that you may be able to*
> *discern what is best and may be pure and blameless until the day*
> *of Christ, filled with the fruit of righteousness that comes through*
> *Jesus Christ—to the glory and praise of God. (Phil. 1:9–11)*

Amen, and amen.

Slow Notes

- Use TiVo to zap commercials and avoid channel surfing. If something sexual does show up, you and your children look—and
  click—away.
- Two words: Internet filter.

- Ask your children what characteristics they would like in an excellent spouse. Then flip it: Ask what characteristics they think they should develop in themselves in order to *be* an excellent spouse. If faithfulness or purity aren't on the list, gently bring it up.

- Evaluate your own media diet using a one to ten scale to rate the sexual content of shows and songs. (One = G-rated; ten = the entire plot/theme is centered on sex.)

- Do the same with your child's favorites. Discuss your findings.

- Ask the Lord to increase your sensitivity to sexual themes.

- Has our highly sexualized society sucked in you or anyone in your family so far that you can't get out? If anyone is struggling with a sexual addiction, get help.

- Dads take note: Studies show that for both sons and daughters, having a close, healthy, and loving relationship with their dad positively affects their view of sex and marriage.

- Discuss your subculture's degree of modesty (e.g., in some churches, people may be more or less concerned about certain attire, and the definition of modesty differs dramatically from region to region and country to country). With your spouse, determine your own family's degree of modesty and discuss it with the kids.

- Explain your limits are own family's rules, and avoid mistaken assumptions that other families' choices are wrong or that the family rule is God's law.

- Girls can use practical tips to evaluate their wardrobes at http://secretkeepergirl.com/Truth_or_Bare.aspx.

- When your son reaches his teens, arrange a coming-of-age retreat led by the significant men in his life. They can discuss the struggles men face and present a meaningful symbol like the popular purity key.

- Arrange a similar event for your daughter with wise women. Consider having Dad or her trusted father figure show up to present a purity ring.
- Chaperone parties. Continually drop in with snacks and drinks.
- Prepare kids in advance to know how to gracefully change the subject or halt an inappropriate conversation with friends.
- Talk about what to do when they find themselves in an uncomfortable situation. Develop a code phrase or text that your kids can use so they can save face—let them blame you for making them come home early (while secretly asking you to rescue them).
- Older kids facing sexual temptation will appreciate this high-speed analogy: *If you don't want to drive over a cliff, you shouldn't pull up to the edge and race the engine.*

Live from the Slow Zone: *Beth Pfister*

My daughter's definition of modesty is *guarding your beauty for just one man.* Basically, we talk about covering your body. Talk about slowing things down—I think you have to start teaching modesty when they're toddlers. I've seen what parents dress their little kids in—outfits with inappropriate phrases printed on the bottoms, or string bikinis at the swimming pool. The parents don't have any standards until their daughter starts to develop, and then the parents freak and want to demand a modesty standard.

There's a disconnect in how you allow your daughter to dress and how you expect her to behave—or how you expect boys to respond to your daughter, with their eyes constantly being drawn to her body. I'll often hear—and this is true—"Well, boys still have to behave and do their part." But the young lady has her part too. I'm tired of people saying, *I should be able to wear whatever I want.*

For the believer, these issues go back to yearning for the Lord. I can preach modesty issues, I can make rules for my children, but what I've tried to do is ask, "Where's the Lord in it?" It's very easy as a parent to just teach rules, but it has to come from a love for the Lord. I've tried to teach modesty from that place—or it does become just about rules. And if it's only a rule, it will never stand. Rules need to start at the heart and be rooted in relationship and a desire to please the Lord. Of course we have to be obedient, but that comes from our love for Him. So if our kids don't have an understanding of His holiness and who He is, then all these things will just be rules.

18 Taking Time to Create

Where in all of our complicated rush and hurry does a kid explore ideas? For families on the run, creativity is often reduced to little more than a black-line coloring sheet and five crayons from the kids' meal bag. Maybe children will scribble during transit times while being shuttled from the Spanish tutor to Kindermusik or Robot Camp, where we parents assume the "real" creativity is happening. Somehow we assume that creativity can be scheduled into a one-hour time slot. And if our child is absorbed in a project, forget it—when time's up, we've got to move on. Sister has cello lessons and brother has baseball.

But researchers claim that meaningful creativity rarely happens on demand or on the go. Innovative thinking, problem solving, experimentation, and focus associated with creativity are hard to achieve when a person is yanked away in the middle of formulating his thoughts. If a child is never given time to focus, ponder his experiences, or make connections, we're robbing him of a critical step in learning and personal development. Research indicates that people need unstructured time to think and create. These minds that God has given us and the ideas we drop into them benefit from entering the simplified pace of the Slow Zone.

"You need the chance to stay with an activity for as long as it captivates your imagination," says Ann Lewin, director of the Capitol

Children's Museum in Washington DC. "A hurry-up culture means that again and again an adult steps in just at that creative moment when a child is heading toward mastery, and ends it.… Children are hurried through their lives without the natural rhythm of unfolding. That, more than anything, will stifle creativity."[1]

Moments of inquiry, discovery, and wonder rarely occur for our kids (or us) in our hurry-up culture. The "natural rhythm of unfolding" is hard to experience at 5000 rpm.

During one of the simpler, slower seasons when our kids were young, we read Bible stories aloud, which they would then retell in various ways. They would act them out in costume or cast Playmobil characters in the roles to re-create the scene. Other times they'd draw the story with colored pencils or markers. What fascinated me most was that when they were given open-ended time later in the day, the stories resurfaced. They wove details and characters into their songs and story lines, and they often arrived—through creative play and expression—at a richer understanding of the story's meaning.

Creativity is a gift from God to be submitted to Him. He can use it as a powerful tool for learning, growth, and understanding. Bright, inquisitive, childlike minds are so open to God's revelation. He gave our children the ability to think, wonder, and question. When we align our thoughts—our creativity—with God's Truth, our minds are renewed, and when we yield to the Lord and remain in step and responsive to His Holy Spirit, we have the potential to produce fresh, innovative, truly inspired ideas.

Writers and researchers have been studying the mind and creative thinking for years and insist that society needs out-of-the-box, innovative problem-solvers to address the increasingly complex issues we face daily. What better source of creative, innovating thinking than a believer accessing the mind of Christ, the truth of His Word, and the power of His Spirit? As our kids pursue Christ, they can experience renewed minds producing creative ideas and solutions that are grounded in truth. What an investment in real learning and promising futures!

Our kids are going to need the confidence and creativity that flows naturally from an active imagination—not only in childhood but into adulthood as well. Whether we realize it or not, we all need to effectively think, solve problems, experiment, and use our imaginations every day while navigating traffic, when at work, or while interacting with friends.

Creativity flourishes in that Slow Zone. To enter? Simplify. Zero in on doing a few things well, and free up some time to embrace and nurture free-form creativity. Say no to something—many things—and learn to set limits.

But people worry about too much freedom: "With no specific purpose planned out, aren't we just setting ourselves up for chaos and outbursts? What's going to happen at a practical level? Don't we need to keep the kids busy? What will we *do?*" Life in the Slow Zone may seem uncomfortable, unproductive, or even meaningless to those accustomed to the fast-paced, complicated life. Free time and slow-motion living can feel like shucking valuable opportunities.

Won't the Kids Just Get Bored?

Maybe they will get bored. But there's great value in a little boredom.

My friend's nine-year-old daughter was invited to a ladies' tea party for her grandmother's birthday on a sunny spring day. One of her aunts, also a friend of mine, sat next to me and spotted the girl through a window.

"Oh, no. She looks bored," she observed. "I feel bad."

"Why?" I asked.

"I hate for her to be bored. She's the only young girl here," she said. "I should find something for her to do."

"Even if she's bored, I think she'll be fine," I offered. I told her that during my childhood I attended countless gatherings populated by much older family members who sat around in rocking chairs swatting flies and swapping stories that were of little interest to me. Sometimes my grandma would find something simple I could play with—I remember spending hours with an inkpad and a box of old rubber stamps pretending I worked at a store. Or she'd pull down the stairs to the attic so that I could spend the afternoon donning old hats and dresses. But often I simply wandered around her yard, lost in thought or inventing an imaginary world. Boredom led to creativity.

"What's the worst that can happen?" I proposed. "If she doesn't figure out something to do, she'll just have one little memory from childhood of being bored at her grandma's birthday tea party. But she's a clever girl. I think she'll come up with something."

The aunt seemed doubtful. We watched her wandering aimlessly around the side yard. This aunt showed loving concern for her niece, wanting life to be fun—and the girl was looking hopelessly bored. Would creativity really kick in?

Much later, after cucumber sandwiches and muffins, someone asked about the girl. Where was she? We looked out a window down at the creek that ran through the property. An older cousin had joined her, and she stood on the bank squishing mud between her toes. Her filmy spring dress flipped against her legs and her dark hair tossed in the breeze. She was throwing pebbles into the water and watching the ripples, some minnows, or a frog. Whatever it was they'd invented, it definitely wasn't boring. They were laughing and full of life.

The aunt—and perhaps a lot of us—seemed to forget that children can entertain themselves with low-tech, simple items. All that was needed that afternoon were some pebbles and the shadowy whisk of minnows slipping around stones in a winding creek.

This isn't an unrealistic, anachronistic idealism I'm touting. I'm not suggesting we turn Luddite and toss out our BlackBerrys or their Nintendos and build a little place in the country cut off from society (though many slow families have). It's possible to live simpler and slower right here and now, creating an environment in which creativity can flourish. That environment can include structure and boundaries that leave plenty of room for creative, focused free-play, but kids will often make it happen on the fly.

One afternoon three of my kids had to wait after school with me as the fourth finished softball practice. I got involved in a long cell phone conversation. The three waiting kids could have sat there, bored, but instead they launched creative free-play. No electronics were involved, no game board with little plastic pieces was necessary, no adult was on the sidelines calling out rules or organizing the activity. Three young kids simply engaged their imaginations on a warm spring day, hopping out of the car and following each other up and over the sidewalk and the curbs, across the grass and

around a big fir tree in a rollicking game of "Follow the Leader."
They made the most of the moment, enjoying spontaneous fun.

When the sister was done with her practice, I called out to the
others, "Come on! Time to go!"

"Awwww," they complained, "do we have to?"

Life can be lived simply. Families can slow down. Not every
moment must be productive, as I must remember as well, when
squeezing in another phone call.

At first, Minivan Kids may have a hard time slowing down.
Accustomed to relaxing with electronics, for example, they may
quickly tire of Play-Doh or dress-up. But before long, kids transition from the adrenaline and pressure of rushing to a slower life of
creativity. Some kids continue to crave some degree of motion and
activity, while others will almost melt naturally and gratefully into
the simpler lifestyle.

Regardless of temperament, however, most young kids given
time and freedom delight in digging for worms or playing Robinson
Crusoe in an untilled garden. A ball of string and a tree or two
can become a force field, a web, or a cordoned-off personal space
that they claim for the afternoon. Stories from school, books, and
Scripture may weave into their free time so that they "own" them at
a depth that's difficult to achieve on the run. They eventually enter
the Slow Zone and dream. They wonder. They generate ideas and
start making connections. They experiment and solve problems
with whatever they undertake. They imagine and take risks, acting
on the curiosity that compels them to explore a topic or idea or
possibility. They concentrate—if we don't yank them away—on the
task at hand.

The speed of creativity is slow. Carve out some time and see what your family dreams up.

Slow Notes

Encourage creativity in your home with some of these supplies and ideas.

- List craft or activity ideas that kids can manage independently as much as possible. Post on the fridge for easy reference. Resource suggestions:
  - *The Family Manager's Guide to Summer Survival: Make the Most of Summer Vacation with Fun Family Activities, Games, and More!* by Kathy Peel.
  - *Summer Fun!: 60 Activities for a Kid-Perfect Summer* (Williamson Kids Can! series includes a science book, Boredom Busters, and a Little Hands series for younger kids) by Susan Williamson.
- Accept a little mess. Show kids where they can spread out their game/toy/artwork/craft/etc. Teach them to contain the mess and clean up afterward.
- Keep raw materials on hand:
  - Old corks
  - Fishing line
  - Good markers that work
  - Colored pencils, crayons, and interesting pens
  - Glue and glue sticks
  - Lots of paper of various sizes and colors

- Rope, clothesline, and string
- Old material
- Shoe boxes, big boxes, and some boxes for cardboard (store them flattened, if need be)
- Washable tempera paint
- Notebooks, blank books, and journals. Collect bright colors and interesting designs on sale after school begins for creative writing projects, diaries, journals, drawing, and cartooning.
- Basic "building block" toys require more imagination than specialized or electronic toys:
  - LEGOs
  - K'NEX
  - Lincoln Logs
  - Playmobil
  - Cardboard bricks or blocks
  - Dolls and doll clothes
  - Toobers and Zots
  - Erector sets
  - Wooden building blocks
- Collect dress-up clothes. Gaudy dresses, cowboy boots, bathrobes, crazy hats, and high heels can augment a collection of Halloween costumes.
- Cameras and camcorders. Set up the tripod for them to invent scenes and plays to record and review. If you can trust older kids to be careful, they can walk around with the equipment to catch close-ups.

Live from the Slow Zone: *Bill Vriesema*

We've chosen to live in more of a farm atmosphere, and choosing to heat with firewood has helped us foster those times together, build memories, and develop stories. This slower lifestyle happens to fit in with some other values that we have, like being out in nature and working together, but you don't need to live on ten acres out in the country and heat with firewood to live a simple life. In some ways it's anything but simple, but cutting and hauling wood is a daily activity that draws us together.

Our kids' friends have noticed that we're different and seem drawn to our home, but it's not because we heat with firewood. I think it's because we've fostered an open, comfortable home that welcomes other people. We're transparent, and kids feel comfortable with us. They are drawn to the openness in our family.

19 The Unhurried Family

One summer afternoon, my then-six-year-old Wondergirl daughter asked for scrap paper. "I need lots of it!" she announced. "And do we have glue?"

I provided her with the requested materials and forgot about it. Later that day I passed through the room where she was working. She was gluing the sheets of paper together, forming a bigger rectangle, wide and long. Chopsticks lined the edges as a type of frame.

"What are you making?" I asked.

"Something," she answered evasively. "A project."

"What kind of project?"

"Just something."

Hmm … an uncharacteristically vague response. She usually loves to provide detailed descriptions of her latest paper creations—an intricately folded chair for a Beanie Baby, say, or a homemade paper backpack she's able to use for two days until it rips. In the past, we've listened to her plans—each snip of the scissors, every swipe of the glue stick, the zigs and zags she'll work into the pattern designed with colored markers.

This time we got nothing. Maybe she was hiding something? I glanced up at Philippe, who happened to be standing nearby. I raised one eyebrow—*what do you think she's up to?* He shrugged and grinned—*it looks harmless enough.*

The next day, while in the car, someone brought up the subject of flight.

"I don't know anyone who can fly," daughter Skeptical said.

"Me neither," daughter Sensibility agreed.

Slight pause.

"I can!" Wondergirl exclaimed. She waited for a response.

"Really?" I asked. "How are you going to do that? In an airplane?"

"You know that project I'm working on with all the scrap paper I'm gluing together?"

"Yes."

She took in a deep breath before blurting out, "I'm making wings!"

Before I figured out what to say next, Skeptical offered a reminder of basic physics. "You have to be light," she stated.

"You're too heavy," Sensibility agreed. "Gravity will pull you back down."

"I'm *going* to fly," Wondergirl insisted. "I just need more paper."

"Well, I've got a lot of paper," I said. "I just came across another big stack last night."

Her enthusiasm was building. "I'm going to need a lot of sheets. And more glue!"

We were quiet for a moment. Then Sensibility spoke up. "It's highly unlikely you will ever fly," she stated firmly.

"I will!" Wondergirl resolved. "I'll fly." In the face of reality and even cynicism, her enthusiasm persisted. By now the others were engaged as well.

Sensibility spoke up again. "Well, if you're making wings," she began, "you should make them out of cardboard. The paper will just rip." Ah, creativity was taking over: Problems were being evaluated with possible solutions. Ideas were formulating as everyone considered the plan.

Wondergirl responded right away. "Cardboard? That's a good idea, because I'll just need scissors for that. I won't need all of that glue."

When we got home that afternoon, Wondergirl and I worked together with kitchen scissors and a big box I had been using for storage. We sized the cardboard to her outstretched arms, and she taped sticks to the underside as handles. They seemed sturdy enough; she was ready to try them out.

She wanted to climb a tree or to the top of our tool shed. "Um, how about you do your trial flight from the top of the slide?" I urged. "It's plenty high for starters."

"Good idea." She climbed up, maneuvering this way and that with those awkward brown rectangles sticking out each side of her slender frame. She positioned herself as high as possible at the top of the small, short yellow slide. With the deep blue summer sky as a backdrop, the sun streaming across her pink T-shirt and purple shorts, she concentrated, began flapping, and jumped.

Plop!

She looked up, a little grin on her face. "I'll try again," she called out. She climbed up again, flapped, and—plop. Plop. Plop. Undaunted, she tried at least four more times. "Maybe I need a little more wind?" she offered.

At some point in the climbing and plopping, a sister showed up to watch. "Maybe we could build a long, wooden ramp that she could run up and then jump off the end."

"Like a runway?" I asked.

"Kind of, except that it would get high at the end."

I was all for creativity, but I didn't think I could construct a wooden ramp. "Nice idea, but we'll have to talk to Papa about that."

The next day I found a library video about flight by David Macauley. Wondergirl came downstairs after watching it and announced that the wings needed to curve more so that air could get under them. She bent them slightly and tried again, but they still didn't work. With each experiment, the wings grew floppier and less promising. Eventually they looked like the Red Baron himself had shot them down.

Wondergirl didn't fly that day, of course, but not for lack of trying. We provided her with key resources for creativity, including plenty of cardboard and time. Obstacles only inspired potential solutions. I suspect she felt some of the same excitement and drive that the Wright Brothers enjoyed during their determined pursuit of flight.

She proved herself persistent and had a great time trying, but at some point she did shelve the project. We recycled the cardboard wings, and she moved on to science experiments with a purple cabbage. One day, however, I suspect she'll try again; just as she announced in the car, she *will* fly.

If we put the brakes on the overcommitted, overextended lifestyle that the world tempts us to pursue, we may watch our children fly in ways we never expected as they discover interests and passions that we merely guessed at when we signed them up for this club or that.

That deep blue summer afternoon affirmed my ongoing struggle and determination to put the brakes on Minivan Mania and preserve the Slow Zone. After all, how can anyone soar when they're strapped into a car seat? Anytime I need inspiration or motivation, I should return to the vivid memory of my six-year-old—free to dream, imagine, create—stretching out two wide cardboard wings against the afternoon sun, ready to soar.

It's countercultural to turn off the TV, say no to a sports team, and send the kids to the backyard with no other instructions than to "go play." We may second-guess ourselves when they mutter, "I'm bored." In fact, we may be tempted to rush off in search of pre-fabricated craft kits and a paint-by-numbers scene, or sign up for a program at the community center.

As a mom committed to maintaining the Slow Zone, I've seen that if my kids are bored for awhile, they eventually do something. They might start small and climb a tree or pick up a stick to swish as a sword. They may gather pinecones and grass and stir up some concoction that they "cook" over an imaginary fire. They aren't bored for long.

There is certainly space in their lives for a few organized sports, camps, or clubs. Music and dance can be rewarding pursuits that lead to lifelong passions. But when we fill our lives to the brim, kids (and even parents) lose out on the importance of free-form creativity. I'd love to see all kids have the time and freedom to squish together mud pies, roll in the sand, build a kite, stage a puppet play, and make a fort out of sheets and clothes pins—ideas they generate, plan, and execute on their own.

All of that takes time. Free time. Unscheduled, spontaneous, experimental moments, or even entire days dedicated to creativity. It takes parents who believe it's worth it to leave some white space in their calendars, vacuum around the LEGO structures, freely pass out the Scotch tape and Elmer's glue, and shower down a mud-caked kid at the end of a summer afternoon.

Enter the Slow Zone and see what takes flight.

Grateful for the Slow Zone

Slowing down isn't the only way to live—families can choose to stay in the fast lane and continue the pace they've known for years. Some people pull it off; some people thrive on it. You might experiment with a slower, unhurried pace of life and realized it's not for you. Perhaps your family can handle a huge capacity, and that's to be celebrated. Stay close to the Lord and your family, and enjoy the ride! God has made some people to sustain a high-speed, high-demand life without suffering any ill effects.

But I'll have to applaud you from the slow lane as you speed off. We've determined our limits and embraced a slower life that fits our family fleet. We'll stay open to change, and if God calls us to take on more, we'll have to trust Him to keep us afloat. Otherwise, we're sticking with the Slow Zone.

But I also want to be sure you know that our unhurried life is imperfect and inconsistent. We're undisciplined by nature, so any discipline we muster up takes a great deal of effort. Were we more structured and organized people, perhaps we could increase our pace without feeling pressured and frantic. We often experiment with ideas that end up kicking us into high gear, and then we have to reorganize ourselves, regroup, and redefine our pace to one that is *slow enough*.

While I'd describe many of our choices as countercultural, we haven't made extreme choices. We haven't yet moved to the country to live off the land, for example, even though a rural setting sometimes reduces urban and suburban temptations to pile on countless extracurricular activities. And we aren't a one-car family.

Still, our lives do seem to be slower than those of most people around us. One thing we have is some "cushion" in our schedule—some "margin." As a result, we're available to people and can be spontaneous. I've started to escort the kids to their piano lessons by bicycle instead of zipping over by van. We don't have cable, and as a result of so few shows to choose from, we watch very little TV, reducing the impact of marketing efforts and freeing up a lot of time. With that time, we do things like plant a vegetable garden in our suburban backyard, pick apples at the local orchard, or read together. We have time to help our neighbors with practical needs as they go through a major medical crisis. So far, we can serve them and still have space in our schedules to take care of ourselves—to be rested and ready to take on what God asks of us.

Probably the most extreme choice we've made is to home educate, though we don't do it every year. Over time we've come to a full appreciation of what it requires, respecting its pros and cons. The years we've kept the kids home, we've reserved time to connect with families so that our kids (and we) build friendships. As they pursue academics, they also develop life skills through meaningful work at home. We've done all of that at a pace that allows for rest as well as sports and hobbies. It's tempting, even as a homeschooled family, to commit to too much—limitless educational opportunities could fill the homeschool day as quickly as anyone else's. We learned that we had to choose to simplify and slow down just as much when we taught at home as when they were enrolled in an institutional setting.

This slower life has not resulted in perfect offspring who never squabble. We irritate each other, grumble, and forget to smile. In spite of Wondergirl's enthusiasm for construction and flight, we don't float around in a state of utter creative delight. We say things we regret and have to apologize. Often.

But life lived more slowly has pulled us together to work as a team. We spend enough time together that we've come to appreciate each other's unique gifts and abilities. We play and work together pretty well and work through things when we don't. I've seen practical ways Philippe and I can impress the Lord's commandments on our children by talking about them when we sit at home with the kids, when we walk along the road, and when we lie down and get up (see Deut. 6:4–7). We are together often, living at a slower pace, able to discuss the truths of God's Word right when we're in the midst of life.

Half the time, though, we don't know what we're doing. We're making this up as we go.

And we're so grateful that God has not left us alone. I sit sometimes and scribble such helpless-sounding entries in my journal. I need Him. Every day I need Jesus to help me discern the next step to take:

Let the morning bring me word of your unfailing love,
for I have put my trust in you.
Show me the way I should go,
for to you I lift up my soul. (Ps. 143:8)

I may always tend toward insecurity and question whether or not I ought to sign the kids up for another dozen activities. If so, I'll need the Lord's ongoing assurance and reminders to stay on this path, the slower path, or I'll slip right back onto the heavily traveled fast lane. It's easy to end up there by default.

I'd love to see you on the slow path as well ... but whatever speed you choose, whatever way you're shown, may your journey take you to quiet places filled with wonder. May you and your children play, laugh, discover, create, celebrate, sing, pray, and worship.

May your family choose to slow down enough to walk with the Lord Jesus Christ ... and give thanks.

Meet the *Live from the Slow Zone* Contributors

Andrea Birch seeks to be a "flourishing mother" (http://flourishing mother.blogspot.com/) for her four children. Her longing for something deeper with the Lord expresses itself in her writing. As a home educator, she enjoys the option of a slower pace of life and has witnessed how that plays out in practical ways. Her observations often inspire me to want to flourish as well.

I've known Susan Clark and her family over eighteen years. She and her husband, Stephen, were missionaries in Belgium for two years, working with the publishing house that Philippe's family helped found, so we share a love of the French language and Belgian baked goods. They returned to the States, and Susan to her work as an obstetric nurse. In that role, Susan assisted the delivery of my fourth child—and let me tell you, that makes her an unusually close friend. Susan and Stephen have three kids between the ages of eight and seventeen.

When Lynn House (mother of four boys) and I first met on our church's communications team, we were two young moms hoping to keep our minds and skills fresh. We can go months without running into each other and then reconnect and spend an hour discussing the Lord and life and a million other things. We share a passion for writing and learning.

Sara Janssen (mother of a three-year-old daughter and a baby on the way) was one of those bloggers who stood out for her radical choices and radical faith. I latched onto her blog (www.walkslowlylivewildly .com) several years ago, visiting often to follow her journey. I mean, who wouldn't be intrigued by a Christian who traveled the United States with her family in an RV that uses recycled vegetable oil as fuel?

I was drawn to the title of Aimee Kollmansberger's blog: Living, Loving, and Learning Simply (http://livinglearningandlovingsimply.blogspot .com). The mother of four children, Aimee has said that her purpose in this stage of life is to love God and others through homemaking and hospitality. Through her kind and positive tone, she offers helpful tips and devotional thoughts as she ponders her simple life.

For years, Beth Pfister (mother of four, ages sixteen to twenty-one) has hosted her kids' teenaged friends on the weekends for pizza nights with devotionals, offering a listening ear. These kids have turned to Beth and her husband, Jeff, for input and advice, so she knows their world well. I've known Beth for years, and I, too, have turned to her for input and advice. Her insight into the world of teens and her strong stances on major issues have stood out as rare and needed in our world.

Rachel Anne Ridge (mother of three, ages fourteen to twenty-one) encourages women through her blog, Home Sanctuary (http://

homesanctuary.typepad.com/), offering a wide range of practical suggestions—everything from small tips for cleaning the toilet and clearing out the hall closet to inspiring kids to help with chores. She shares a wealth of information, tossed out daily to Internet readers in a light and friendly tone.

Trish Southard (mother of one daughter, age twelve) and I have been friends since 1993. This classy lady models a walk of faith, exemplified when she left her career when her husband, Todd, felt called to attend seminary and enter ministry full-time. Now she leads women's ministry at her church, mentors women, speaks, leads book clubs, and has continued to offer valuable insight to my writing … and ongoing support as a friend.

Sharon Stohler and I met when we both began home educating our preschool-age children who are now teens. Over the years, her wisdom and skill as a trained schoolteacher have been instrumental in sharpening me as a mom and educator. She's also faithfully prayed with and for me, naturally sharing her rich, intimate, obedient faith in Jesus Christ. Sharon and her husband, Ron, a pastor, have three kids between the ages of nine and fifteen.

Gia Tubbs (mother of four, ages four to seventeen) and I met several years ago when our kids attended a small private school. I was drawn to Gia's soft, sweet spirit. Since then, we've both transitioned to homeschooling and ended up at the same church, so we overlap more and more—our kids sang in the church Christmas concert, and come to think of it, my son needs to return a gray LEGO that he absentmindedly stuck in his pocket when playing at their house.

When I clicked on Ann Voskamp's blog (www.aholyexperience.com), I entered an online oasis. Visually and verbally, Ann has created a space that invites readers to pause and reflect. A contemplative mom with a gift of poetic insight, Ann leads her readers to a slow, rich world of deeper thought, wonder, and beauty. She and her husband home educate their six kids (ages three to thirteen) on their Canadian farm.

I met Bill & Judy Vriesema (parents of three kids, ages eighteen to twenty-one) several years ago at a Christian family camp. Because their delightful, creative, respectful, bright, and friendly family left a powerful impression, I've picked their brains for parenting advice, taking copious notes. Vriesema trivia—the tiring task of heating their log house exclusively with wood has been far from simple, but it requires steps that led to healthy family communication and teamwork.

Notes

Introduction

1. Mark Buchanan, *The Rest of God: Restoring Your Soul by Restoring Sabbath* (Nashville: W Publishing Group, 2006), 45.
2. Pew Research Center, "Inside the Middle Class: Bad Times Hit the Good Life," Social and Demographic Trends, April 9, 2008, http://pewsocialtrends.org/pubs/706/middle-class-poll (accessed January 7, 2009).

Chapter 1: What Are We Missing Out On?

1. Gene Weingarten, "Pearls Before Breakfast," *Washington Post*, April 8, 2007, http://www.washingtonpost.com/wp-dyn/content/article/2007/04/04/AR2007040401721.html (accessed May 23, 2008).
2. Ibid.
3. Elizabeth Barrett Browning, "Seventh Book," *Aurora Leigh* (New York: T.Y. Crowell, 1883), 265.
4. Ann Voskamp, "Still Songs," A Holy Experience Blog, April 17, 2008, http://aholyexperience.com/2008/04/still-songs.html (accessed January 7, 2009).

Chapter 2: What's the Hurry?

1. Girl Scouts, "Insignia List," http://www.girlscouts.org/program/ gs_central/insignia/list/ (accessed January 7, 2009).
2. Ken Gire, *The Reflective Life* (Colorado Springs: Chariot Victor, 1998), 99.
3. Audrey Barrick, "Survey: Christians Too Busy for God," *Christian Today*, July 31, 2007, http://www.christiantoday.com/article/survey .christians.too.busy.for.god/11977.htm (accessed March 17, 2009).
4. Ibid.
5. John E. Johnson, "Slow Down, Don't Move So Fast: Our Pace Has Costs," *The Oregonian*, June 24, 2000.
6. John Ortberg, *The Life You've Always Wanted* (Grand Rapids, MI: Zondervan, 1997), 81.
7. Ibid., 82.

Chapter 3: How Did We Get Here?

1. Aimee Kollmansberger, "Making Your Day Simple," Living, Learning, and Loving Simply Blog, September 26, 2007, http:// livinglearningandlovingsimply.blogspot.com/2007_09_01_archive.html (accessed January 7, 2009).

Chapter 4: What Are We Trying to Achieve?

1. Dr. Tim Kimmel, *Raising Kids for True Greatness: Redefine Success for You and Your Child* (Nashville: W Publishing Group, 2006), xi, 37.

Chapter 5: Slowing Down Childhood

1. Harry R. Lewis, "Slow Down: Getting More out of Harvard by Doing Less," Harvard College, January 9, 2004, http://www.eecs.harvard.edu/~lewis/SlowDown2004.pdf (accessed January 7, 2009).

2. Benedict H. Gross, Harvard College, "Communications from the Dean: Welcome Letter to the Class of 2009," August 2005, http://www.college.harvard.edu/deans_office/communications/61.html (accessed January 7, 2009).

3. William Fitzsimmons, Marlyn E. McGrath, and Charles Ducey, "Time Out or Burn Out for the Next Generation," Harvard College, rev. ed. 2006, http://www.admissions.college.harvard.edu/prospective/applying/time_off/timeoff.html (accessed January 7, 2009).

Chapter 6: Too Fast to Care

1. Richard Beck, "Everyday Evil, Part 6: Hurry," Experimental Theology Blog, http://experimentaltheology.blogspot.com/2007/09/everyday-evil-part-6-hurry.html (accessed January 7, 2009).

2. Ibid.

3. Ibid.

4. J. M. Darley and C. D. Batson, "'From Jerusalem to Jericho': A Study of Situational and Dispositional Variables in Helping Behavior," *Journal of Personality and Social Psychology* 27 (1973), http://faculty.babson.edu/krollag/org_site/soc_psych/darley_samarit.html (accessed January 7, 2009).

5. Beck, "Everyday Evil, Part 6: Hurry."

Chapter 7: Too Fast to Rest

1. Po Bronson, "Snooze or Lose," *New York Magazine,* October 8, 2007, http://nymag.com/news/features/38951 (accessed January 7, 2009).
2. Ibid.
3. Ibid.
4. Ibid.
5. Ibid.
6. Buchanan, *The Rest of God,* 36 (see introduction, n. 1).
7. Ibid., 40.
8. Andrea Birch, "Emotional and mental rest on the Sabbath," The Flourishing Mother Blog, April 27, 2008, http://flourishingmother. blogspot.com/2008/04/emotional-and-mental-rest-on-sabbath.html.

Chapter 9: Too Fast to Pray or Worship

1. Carl Gustav Boberg, "How Great Thou Art."

Chapter 10: Load Limits

1. National Maritime Museum, "Ships, seafarers & life at sea," National Maritime Museum, http://www.nmm.ac.uk/explore/sea-and-ships/facts/ships-and-seafarers/load-lines (accessed March 18, 2009).
2. Dr. Richard A. Swenson, *The Overload Syndrome: Learning to Live Within Your Limits* (Colorado Springs: NavPress, 1998), 27.
3. The basic idea of the ship analogy used here originated in a message by Jill Briscoe in the 1980s, given to a women's group in Liberia. My friend Ruth Van Reken later passed the story down to me. I have built upon that idea considerably over the years, using my own research and observations.

4. Tom Harris, "How Aircraft Carriers Work," HowStuffWorks.com, August 29, 2002, http://science.howstuffworks.com/aircraft-carrier.htm (accessed March 25, 2009).

5. *Encyclopaedia Britannica Online*, s.v. "Cargo Ship," http://www .britannica.com/EBchecked/topic/95751/cargo-ship (accessed March 25, 2009).

6. "Barge," Maritime Connector, http://www.maritime-connector.com/ ContentDetails/77/gcgid/80/lang/English/Barge.wshtml (accessed March 25, 2009).

7. Wikipedia contributors, "Tugboat," *Wikipedia, The Free Encyclopedia*, http://en.wikipedia.org/wiki/Tugboat (accessed March 25, 2009).

8. Ford Walpole, "Living For Shrimping, Shrimping For A Living," *South Carolina Wildlife*, May/June 2007, http://www.scwildlife .com/pubs/mayjune2007/shrimping.html (accessed March 25, 2009).

9. Victor Epand, "Sailboats: Fun in Many Forms," *Ezine*, http:// ezinearticles.com/?Sailboats---Fun-in-Many-Forms&id=1606876 (accessed March 25, 2009)

10. Wikipedia contributors, "Destroyer," *Wikipedia, The Free Encyclopedia*, http://en.wikipedia.org/wiki/Destroyer (accessed March 25, 2009).

11. Leonard Roueche, "Ferries," *The Canadian Encyclopedia*, "Ferries," http://www.thecanadianencyclopedia.com/index.cfm?PgNm=TCE&Pa rams=A1ARTA0002774 (accessed March 25, 2009).

12. Wikipedia contributors, "Dinghy," *Wikipedia, The Free Encyclopedia*, http://en.wikipedia.org/wiki/Dinghy (accessed March 25, 2009).

13. "Boat and Yacht Types Explained," Croatia Charter, http://www. croatiacharter.com/boats.asp (accessed March 25, 2009).

Chapter 11: Forget the Joneses

1. Oswald Chambers, *My Utmost for His Highest* (New York: Dodd, Mead & Company, 1935), 270.

2. Rachel Anne Ridge, "Kids' Sports and the Simpler Life," Home Sanctuary Blog, April 18, 2007, http://homesanctuary.typepad.com/ rachelanne/2007/04/choosing_kids_s.html (accessed January 7, 2009).

Chapter 12: Slow Enough to Savor Traditions

1. Mary Pipher, *The Shelter of Each Other* (New York: G.P. Putnam's Sons, 1996), 148.

Chapter 13: Living at the Speed of Love

1. Dr. Gary Chapman, "Learn the Languages: The Five Love Languages," The Five Love Languages, http://www .fivelovelanguages.com/learn.html (accessed January 7, 2009).
2. Lynn House, "Moving at the Speed of Jaden," Lynn's Addiction Blog, September 26, 2007, http://lynnhouse.wordpress.com/ 2007/09/26/ moving-at-the-speed-of-jaden (accessed March 25, 2009).

Chapter 14: High Cost of High Tech

1. Mike Woodruff (pastor of Christ Church Lake Forest), unpublished article.
2. "Television and Health," Internet Resources to Accompany *The Sourcebook for Teaching Science,* http://www.csun.edu/science/health/ docs/tv&health.html (accessed January 7, 2009).
3. Jane E. Brody, "TV's Toll on Young Minds and Bodies," *New York Times*, April 3, 2004, http://www.nytimes.com/2004/08/03/health/ personal-health-tv-s-toll-on-young-minds-and-bodies.html (accessed May 14, 2009).

4. Lesia Oesterreich, "Getting Along: Taming the TV," National Network for Child Care, August 1998, http://www.nncc.org/Parent/ga.tv.html (accessed January 7, 2009).

5. "Television and Health," Internet Resources to Accompany *The Sourcebook for Teaching Science*.

6. "Children and Media Violence," National Institute on Media and the Family, rev. November 2006, http://www.mediafamily.org/facts/facts_vlent.shtml (accessed January 7, 2009).

7. "Television and Health," Internet Resources to Accompany *The Sourcebook for Teaching Science*.

8. Ibid.

9. Ed Wallace, "Television and Nutrition in Juvenile Detention Centers," *Californian Journal of Health Promotion* 3, no. 2 (2005), http://www.csuchico.edu/cjhp/3/2/125-129-wallace.pdf (accessed January 7, 2009).

10. Mary L. Gavin, ed., "How TV Affects Your Child," KidsHealth: For Parents, The Nemours Foundation, October 2008, http://kidshealth.org/parent/positive/family/tv_affects_child.html (accessed January 7, 2009).

11. Ibid.

12. Ibid.

13. Amy B. Jordan, James C. Hersey, Judith A. McDivitt, and Carrie D. Heitzler, "Reducing Children's Television-Viewing Time: A Qualitative Study of Parents and Their Children," *Pediatrics* 118, no. 5 (November 2006), http://pediatrics.aappublications.org/cgi/content/abstract/118/5/e1303 (accessed January 7, 2009).

14. Rhonda Handlon, "Media Violence Study," Focus on the Family, http://www.focusonthefamily.com/entertainment/mediawise/media_awareness/media_violence_study.aspx (accessed January 7, 2009).

15. Bernard Farrales, "Violence in Video Games," March 8, 2002, http://cseserv.engr.scu.edu/StudentWebPages/BFarrales/ResearchPaper.htm (accessed January 7, 2009).

16. Christina Glaubke, Patti Miller, A. McCrae Parker, and Eileen
    Espejo, "Fair Play? Violence, Gender and Race in Video Games,"
    Children Now (December 2001), http://eric.ed.gov/ERICWebPortal/
    contentdelivery/servlet/ERICServlet?accno=ED463092 (accessed
    January 7, 2009).
17. Olivia and Kurt Bruner, "Digital Junkies: Protect Your Child from
    Video-Game Addiction," *Focus on the Family*, Parents Edition, October
    2007, 24.
18. Ibid.
19. Ibid.
20. Ibid.
21. Ibid., 26.
22. Ibid.

Chapter 15: Speeding Past Creation

1. Donna St. George, "Getting Lost in the Great Indoors," *Washington
   Post*, June 19, 2007, http://www.washingtonpost.com/wp-dyn/content/
   article/2007/06/18/AR2007061801808_pf.html (accessed January 7,
   2009).
2. Ruth A. Wilson, "The Wonders of Nature: Honoring Children's Ways
   of Knowing," Earlychildhood NEWS, http://www.earlychildhoodnews.
   com/earlychildhood/article_view.aspx?ArticleID=70 (accessed January
   7, 2009).
3. Rachel Carson, *The Sense of Wonder* (New York: Harper & Row
   Publishers, 1956).
4. Donna St. George, "Getting Lost in the Great Indoors."

Chapter 16: Slowing Down Spending

1. Susan Linn, *Consuming Kids: The Hostile Takeover of Childhood* (New York: New Press, 2004), 35.
2. Ibid., 39.
3. "Facts about Marketing to Children," New American Dream, http://www.newdream.org/kids/facts.php (accessed January 7, 2009).
4. "New Study Reports Children's Exposure to Advertising is Making Them Sick," New American Dream, http://www.newdream.org/kids/borntobuy.php (accessed January 7, 2009).
5. "Facts about Marketing to Children," New American Dream.
6. Ibid.
7. "About Us: Fast Facts," Channel One Network, http://www.channelonenetwork.com/corporate/fast_facts.html (accessed January 7, 2009).
8. Helen Lemmel, "Turn Your Eyes Upon Jesus," 1922.
9. See www.etsy.com.
10. Sara Janssen, "The Compact Revisited," Walk Slowly Live Wildly Blog, http://walkslowlylivewildly.com/2008/03/17/the-compact-revisited/ (accessed January 7, 2009).

Chapter 17: Slowing Down Sexuality

1. Martha Irvine, "10 is the New 15 as kids grow up faster," *USA Today*, November 25, 2006, http://www.usatoday.com/news/health/2006-11-25-teen-tweens_x.htm (accessed January 7, 2009).
2. Laurie Meyers, "Dangerous Dolls?" *Monitor on Psychology* 37, no. 8 (September 2006), http://www.apa.org/monitor/sep06/dolls.html (accessed January 7, 2009).
3. Mary E. DeMuth, *Authentic Parenting in a Postmodern Culture: Practical Help for Shaping Your Children's Hearts, Minds, and Souls* (Eugene, OR: Harvest House, 2007), 28.

4. Ibid.

5. Jane D. Brown, Carolyn Tucker Halpern, Kelly Ladin L'Engle, "Mass Media as a Sexual Super Peer for Early Maturing Girls," *Journal of Adolescent Health* vol. 36, issue 5 (2005): 420-427

6. Carol J. Pardun and Kathy Roberts Forde, "Sexual Content of Television Commercials Watched by Early Adolescents," in *Sex in Consumer Culture,* ed. Tom Reichert and Jacqueline Lambiase. (Philadelphia, PA: Lawrence Erlbaum Associates, 2005), http://www. unc.edu/depts/jomc/teenmedia/pdf/Pardun.pdf (accessed January 7, 2009).

7. Diane Levin, Carol Pardun, and Deborah Roffman, "Media, Sex and Talking to Tweens," interview by Lynn Neary, *Talk of the Nation,* NPR, August 7, 2006, http://www.npr.org/templates/story/story. php?storyId=5624000 (accessed January 7, 2009).

Chapter 18: Taking Time to Create

1. Daniel Goleman, Paul Kaufman, and Michael Ray, *The Creative Spirit* (New York: Plume, 1993), 64.

Resources for
Growing Godly Kids

Revolutionary Parenting
Workbook & Leader's Edition with DVD
George Barna & Karen Lee-Thorp

Based on George Barna's best-selling book, *Revolutionary Parenting*, this interactive workbook and DVD helps parents and family groups move from insight to application. Guided by Barna, readers create a unique plan for growing their own spiritual champions. A great resource for small groups!

Workbook ISBN 978-1-4347-6699-1
Leader's Edition ISBN 978-1-4347-6612-0

Raising a Modern-Day Joseph
Larry Fowler

Drawing from the timeless story of Joseph, author Larry Fowler (executive director of global training for Awana) offers a biblical plan for growing children who will love and serve Jesus Christ. An essential guide for parents, children's ministry workers, and youth leaders.

ISBN 978-1-4347-6705-9

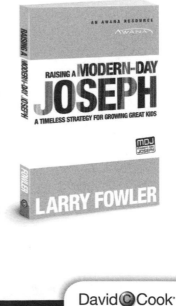

To learn more visit our Web site or a
Christian bookstore near you.

David **C** Cook
transforming lives together

800.323.7543 • DavidCCook.com